Lawrence Johns

Beyond Exile

Beyond Exile

First Edition

No. ____

Book & Cover Design
Author Photograph
Minerva Designs

Front Cover Photograph
SOHO (ESA & NASA)

For Clarence

Beyond Exile

© 2008 by Lawrence Johns

All Rights Reserved

No part of this publication may be reproduced or transmitted in any form or by any means, electronic or mechanical, including photocopy, fax, email or recording, or any information storage and retrieval system, including computers, servers, the internet or world wide web, without permission in writing from the publisher.

Beyond Exile was first published online in serial form by *Void Magazine* in the spring of 2007, with an interpretive photo essay by Rachel Edelman.

ISBN: 9781929096046

Conscious Publishing
2034 SW Vermont Street
Portland, OR 97219

www.consciouspublishing.com

I know how men in exile feed on dreams

Aeschylus

Beyond Exile

That's The Way It Is

They escape to the High Sierras

Bumpy back roads from Nevada side

Listening to the Mozart of swift-dropping streams

Making love in mossy hollows

Sheltered from the mad sting of Memory

But now Heraclitus is jealous

Sprinting for the lakeside boulders

And when Frank comes

He's thinking

Of his dog

Now

Erin

Knows

Her Red King

Is approaching the end of his reign

In cool parenthesis

She watches him dress

Watches Heraclitus rush up

And drop a white owl at her feet

This is the image

Introducing the final frames

Now she believes camping is a bore

She's sick of hardluck stories around the fire

Sick of hippie refugees from the Haight

Tired of eating acid for breakfast

To hear the jazz of morning clouds

Now she shadows the caravans

Looking for a strong new consort

Stops giving the dog scraps

Stops conceding the moment

To feed some momentous Future

Now she's vegetarian

And Frank hides his pain

As he swaps grass

For Porterhouse bones

And bowls of Dinty's beef stew

Now the mountains are too furious

To protect the exhilarating trails

That carried their romance

Erin calls her father

The Navy admiral in San Diego

She's registered pre-law

At the University Of Oregon

She's got a duplex

Three blocks south of campus

2042 Onyx

It's rough snow at Mt Shasta

Stuck two hours while it's plowed ahead

Lighting a Sherman's in the frigid air

She says she's never wanted kids

That's the way it is

Maybe you should get a job Frank

Reality is what happens when First Will hits the Wall

When it becomes Second and Third Will

Reality is recoil Frank

The Light of the Revolution has failed

Love and Hate have decomposed

Deconstructed

We must adapt to adaptive Life

It's insane to go on fighting

When everything is lost

And nobody cares

Rikki

Sammy

Parker

Feather

The Diggers are dead

The Haight is dead

The Counterculture is dead

The Revolution died at People's Park

Kent State

Now it's about survival

It's all about Me

If we don't rejoin Society

Their sacrifices will be forgotten

In our demise

You're in denial Frank

You fight

Because you don't know what else to do

Nixon's in the White House

Disco and porno dictate fashion

Terrorism conditions thought

It's time to get a career

You can't be a Lone Wolf forever

Not forever

How can he recover from these cold shots?

Erin's his Love

His Destiny

Only now does he understand

How much he wants a son

Erin's his beautiful Cosmic Wife

So why doesn't she want kids?

If it's the Truth

His natural instinct was off

And every dawning day

Tracks back to delusion

If it's a Lie

She's decided to knife him

In the liver that never heals

And there's nothing more to say

The Face Of Pythagoras

He knows the Chinese

When they write eight-leg Poetry

He feels this space

Calling that character over

He's been working for months

On nature sketches

And now he's ready

To be the Way

He unwraps the graph paper

And lines up the magic markers

It's late June in Eugene

He has the bright morning sun at thirty degrees

Slanting across the breakfast table

He has Mind transforming itself

Into pure information

The complete history of human Life

Without the interpretations or interpolations

Of a mother tongue

It's knocking

It's here

So he drops the connection

From brain to hand

Lets the numbers rise from the boiling iron

At the spinning center of the Earth

And drop perfectly into the squares

On the lime-green page

See

Each symbol is magnetically imprinted

With the face of Pythagoras

All creation is volcanic

Frank says to a future Frank

There's no writer

There's no writing

There's only Position

That rare and intricate moment

When one leg of the Mystery

Feels like dancing with the other seven

Spencer's Butte

It's five weeks of arguments and sleeplessness

Buried in snowdrifts and sorry excuses

When Erin shows her Beatle boots

Chewed through the toes

I'm going for a drive says Frank

Knowing the van hasn't started in a month

It's got ice to the fenderwells

And the battery's probably dead

Erin gives him a hard look

That irrevocably says

It's Him Or Me

Frank's procrastinated summer

Blocked out the crisp Oregon fall

Heraclitus curls at his ankles

Pretending all is well

But now it's here

Herc stay

Stay

He's shoveling long arcs of dirty snow

Making fat tracks to the street

When Erin opens the front door

Heraclitus tries to slip through the crack

So she kicks him in the snout

And shock

Clamps

Frank's anxious heart

He wants to comfort his dog

He's always comforted his dog

But Erin's pointing to the ignition

And in hideous miracle

The Ford starts

They're rolling

Sliding

Up Onyx

When Frank feels something

Break deep in his Being

Checking the sideview mirror

He sees Heraclitus

Running rabid after the van

His dog never chases cars

His dog's gone mad

As Frank makes a panic right

A blue Chevy station wagon without hubcaps

Loses control at the frozen intersection

Sweeps a wide hook of powder

And kills his best friend at the curb

The driver's holding a red stocking cap

Mumbling he never saw him

Never

Saw

Him

Frank lifts the warm corpse

And puts it back

With the rusty shovel

The snow chains

The sagging old newspapers

Denied recycling

After two numb blocks

He hears Heraclitus

Everywhere

Nowhere

It's OK

I couldn't live without the team

We made it through so many things

But we couldn't get through this woman

It's OK

Frank's shaking

Heraclitus from the Other Side

Refutes his most intimate Philosophy

He drives up Spencer's Butte

Slow grinding the steep grade

As his merciless White Goddess

Of the waning moon

Sharpens her double-bladed ax

In the shotgun seat

Frank slides to a stop

Icy

Empty parking lot

High to his left is the peak

Where he once dropped Mr Natural

Swallowed the setting sun

And became a Hindu dancing girl

Happy with every upspinning blush of the horizon

But the frame of reference isn't the story

The map isn't the territory

Reality is shock and more shock

So he carries Heraclitus to a clearing

With a good view of the valley

And buries him in a deep rocky grave

To frustrate the coyotes

At the last shovel of black loam

It begins to snow again

Glittering white plasma covers his tracks

His paralysis of action passes

He wakes up

To waking up

Married in ecstasy

Divorced in distress

It's not your fault

He's OK

I know she says

He's ascended

Frank drives silent down to Onyx

Collects his things in a travel bag

And twenty minutes later

He's south on I-5

Crying fierce

As he passes Peterbilts on the slick uphill turns

Headed back to Berkeley

The Comprehensives

While he was in Oregon

GTU fired the administration

And gutted the department

Of Theology And The Arts

He was no longer Union Poet

He had to graduate in the traditional manner

His book of numbers was rejected as a dissertation

And he has to stand for comprehensives

With seven world-famous professors

He'd never met

Church history

Systematic theology

And worse

It's vaudeville

Slapstick

The way Frank mugs and dances

Coughing up pebbles from the muddy stream

Of five hundred books

Read seven seconds

A page

He's the Tightrope Walker

The Man Of A Thousand Resources

Improvising context and analysis

In a room of cynical theological orthodoxy

They know he never attended a class

They applaud his scholarly audacity

They note the preface to his numbers book

Was renamed The Will To Greater Orgasm

By the Jesuits

And distributed free on campus

By the Unitarians

They say

T J J Altizer called

And quickly failed him without prejudice

Thanksgiving Light

After his collapse

Jackson was Nietzsche subdued and serene

For three four months

Receiving Italian scholars in a small room

Behind the incessant hurtling machines

Of a Chinese dry cleaner in North Beach

One last medium starched shirt

And Jackson reverts to being Jackson

Providing hot tickets to cabbies

For a cut of strip shows and rooms by the minute

The pressbox at Giants' games

Castro Street after midnight

Then inexplicably in Oregon

Stripping bark from yew trees

For a new cancer cure

He's shot in the ass

By a farmer who maybe owns the land

Maybe finds a cute nurse at the hospital

Hanging coffee shops west of campus

The French-looking dandy with the black beret

And three-o'clock shadow

The plump little blonde

Giggling at every pun and innuendo

When they go wrong

AP immediately picks it up

It's in The Oregonian

The San Francisco Chronicle

The Los Angeles Times

Jackson's busted in Eugene

For coming through the bathroom window

Attempted rape says the judge

You can tell by his greasy fingerprints

On the toilet lid

It's another clear case of Beatle lyrics

The restraining order is for her boyfriend

But looks transferable to me

Take him to Salem

Let's see if he makes trial

Jackson's given electroshock

Rock around the clock in a padded cell

The big red and blue pills

Kesey zoomed in One Flew Over

He's discharged six months later

At 4 in the morning

Spittle running over his lower lip

Apologies bouncing in a broken mind

Toby finds him on the curb after a Berkeley collision

At the southwest corner of Hearst and Oxford

Bleeding badly from the head

Back from the hospital

In a twisted wheelchair and thin Navy blankets

Jackson sleeps for thirteen days

Rising only to piss comatose

It's Thanksgiving

A special light

Vibrates the spidery corners of the kitchen

The turkey's been roasting since 6

Basted with Dimple and hard cider

The smell attracts Toby's crew

Smoking hothouse grass

And dangling bottles of Miller's High Life

Toby's checking the temperature plug

When Jackson appears as The Black Pope

Blessing his faithful assembly

He dismisses the aluminum foil

With a swipe of long yellow fingernails

Strips the carcass of skin

And gulps it down like St Pelican

They're in the presence of The Last Hunger

Witnessing the End of a Gentleman

Hypnotized by the pink nakedness of the turkey

And the certainty

This

Will never happen to them

The boys clap cautiously

Then raucously

Jackson burps

Bows to the refrigerator

And goosesteps back to bed

It's his last magick trick

Three four days later

Toby and Frank wheel him up a steel ramp

Connecting a night flight from Oakland to Atlanta

Where maybe his mother is waiting

The Recurring Dream

Frank's running his white Caddy up the Rose Garden

When he sees two police cruisers

Rushing massive in the rearview mirror

Two more powersliding ahead

Toby's at the passenger window

Shaking out a baggie

Walking badger free

As they spreadeagle Frank on the trunk

Pat him down

Bang his head on the post

And take him to University Station

He's shoved in a cell

With a cracked seatless toilet

Metalmesh bed

He paces for an hour

Analyzing his mistakes

Then lies down on the empty diamonds

And rejoins his recurring dream

It starts with the fight

The day he came home from Leningrad

His father's right cross grazes his jaw

Left uppercut to the stomach

Bulled out the front door

And thrown sprawling on the lawn

For his new Communist beard

His mother crying

His younger brother and sisters

Staring

Learning

The way kids learn

He walks down to Magnolia Avenue

With his Russian sports bag

Retracing the route to Ramona High

Kicked out of the house

Stripped of mother and siblings

By his father in political rage

He's alone

Grandfather was killed

Three years ago

Kicked in the chest by a favorite filly

Grandfather was the one

Who taught him how to be a man

A boy knows

Without knowing

This is where all knowledge starts

His father's an intelligent imposter

His primary motivation

Is fear of failure

His most apparent satisfaction

Is tyrannizing the wife and kids

So

The fight makes it official

Frank's liberated from Family

He'll live on the wind

His wits

Women and friends

He'll turn Exile into Art

But nothing erases this insult

And his dreams soon reflect

A mounting desire for revenge

In the recurring dream he kills his father

By monkeying with the brakes

This rings true

Because he knows little of cars

And nothing of brakes

In the dream he's in jail

Solitary

A cracked seatless toilet

Metalmesh bed

Twenty to life for patricide

He's also elsewhere

Walking the World

Thinking

Strategizing

Investigating the flame of Gnosis

The all-so-material Hate of Material

In this Other Life

He sometimes wakes in a cold sweat

Thinking Owl Creek

He never murdered his father

Never went to jail

But hanging on the bridge increases his anxiety

Until he craves any plausible certainty

Which dream is dominant?

Did Oedipus only imagine his patricide?

What about the blindness?

What about Colonus?

Who really monkeyed with the brakes?

When he was young

And his mother whispered of divorce

He suggested a lawyer

He felt her suffering and helplessness

Her need of cultured friends

Of Art and Opera

But his sisters were small

She thought it best to wait

They embraced

And Frank kissed her

Tasted her

His sperm flowing over her breasts

Like first milk

He has no protection from this dream

It stays away for months

Then invades him five nights in a row

He hates the Freudian touch

His hunger for Vengeance

Must never jeopardize his Freedom

Jail is his UnConscious Mind

Juggling the Undone with the Undead

He'll confound the Oracle

He'll go abroad

As far from his father as he can

But now he wakes from his dream

In a cell beneath Administration

Close to the spot

Where Savio coined Free Speech

It's dawning

As Sergeant Tipton and Captain Poole

Take him to the interrogation room

What's the charge?

GTA says Captain Poole

What?

The plates to the car you're driving

Are registered to one Harvey Phillips says Tipton

And his wife Alicia

Reported it stolen at 8 says Poole

You're busting me for stealing my own car?

It's not your car says Tipton

One Harvey Phillips says Poole

His wife Alicia says Tipton

We know what you're working says Poole

They're searching the car as we speak

They'll find the drugs and plastique

Then you'll be some gorilla's lifetime hole

Unless you cooperate

The officers are temporizing

Trying to gauge his reactions

Signaling to the suits in the mirror

Finger

To

Ear

When Frank laughs low

It's not the dream!

What? says Tipton

Do you want to make a statement? asks Poole

Before disappearing

Frank laughs again

Remembering how Toby sauntered away

Singing Hank Williams

Is this where I demand a lawyer?

Shall I confess to conspiracy?

Shall I explain to the Berkeley Police

The sordid story of LBJ

And what he told his mistress

The night before Dallas?

Shall I introduce Bierce?

It's not your car says Tipton

Before disappearing

Frank's sitting on the table

Whistling Move It On Over

When he feels a tap on the shoulder

It's Dessy

Short brown hair

Charcoal business suit

A Black Star blazing her lapel

I apologize for any inconvenience Frank

It looks like we have the wrong man

She pronounces his name so sensually

It sounds Romanian

The wrong car says Frank quickly

Reading the danger well

Dessy's changed

And stayed impeccably the same

She always was reptilian

But now her lips echo rotten flesh

Her tongue flicks hidden sources of heat

And she never blinks

She's become what she is

How are you Frank?

I resigned

I'm fine

We'll need to know each other better

You'll have a top assignment

And I'm your contact

Remember

I'm the only one who doesn't betray you

That's all

You

Can

Go

Dessy accompanies the command

With a look

Linking erotic obsession

To professional contempt

Officially you're under bench probation

For GTA and resisting arrest

Refrain from stealing tins of smoked oysters

From the Northside Market

Be careful crossing Telegraph at night

And on your best behavior

When Sergeant Tipton calls she says

Before disappearing

Frank's immediately on his feet

Flexing

Stretching

Looking for the trap

He still has his wallet and keys

The steel door's open

So he walks Spanish up the steps

To Sproul Plaza

Observing with reborn pleasure

The Brownian motion

Of bustling coeds

Headed for first-period class

Until his spine

Starts

Rattling

Like a thousand ice cubes

From the surprise touch

Of Kali

Wildflowers

Toby lays the bouquet of wildflowers

On the fused stream of rubber

That fills this tight canyon

In the Bin Hinnom Valley

The San Francisco Chronicle claims

The Air Force shot down a UFO buzzing Livermore

And the crash ignited a used tire depot

The twenty-acre fire blazed nineteen days

You could see the oily plume from Redding

But Toby knows better

On this day Dessy burned Feather at the stake

And torched the depot for cover

On this day Toby curses the Abrahamic God

And vows to heal the World

Before

He heals himself

The Plastic Sax

Hardcastle's thick with hustlers

And the heady roar of gambit blitz

So Frank takes to playing Hardy

At the tranquil UC Student Union

Essaying the Queen's Gambit

With incremental consolidation of Space

And conversations revolving on the gas giants

Today Hardy has a plastic sax

Like the one Charlie Parker found in a pawnshop

For the concert with Dizzy in Toronto

After nineteen moves

They agree to a grandmaster draw

And Hardy's blowing with the drummers

Outside The Bear's Lair

When a diminutive Rastafarian

Asks him to quit

You stink man

Lay off

Hardy keeps going

Grinning divine

And gets slugged

His jaw's broken in eight places

His nose a soft right turn

The surgery and rehabilitation bills follow him

To his mother's garage in Monterey Park

Where he sets up old doors on crates

Writes 22 novels

11 books of astrology

88 film treatments

44 screenplays

And fifty square feet of short stories

Trying to keep Bird from buying that sax

The Smiley Introductions

Kingfish still looks the Black babyface pimp

Ten years into marriage with three kids

Supporting the family with coke and heroin

Blowing off steam with a little poker

Little home seven-stud with Frank

The White rock from the Key Club

They play Mondays

And anytime Kingfish is flush

It's a lucky tune-up

For the big money Friday games

With the dealers and DEA agents

In his cloaked social circle

The bill or two Kingfish drops to Frank

Is handsomely recovered in these high stakes tussles

Where bodyguards with uzis slump the walls

And natural hands never take the monster pots

He's got a present for Frank tonight

A tall Englishman with long brown hair

Aquiline nose

And John Lennon glasses

Found wandering in Fruitvale

With a bad address and no survival skills

Kingfish bought him from Badd Buster Cox

For $50

Thinking he might be good for something

Someday

So it's smiley introductions tonight

Tony's read Philosophy at Cambridge

His father's the Under Secretary Of Health

He's been traveling in the States

For nine months without a nickel

Frank and Tony

Leap

Into Socratic dialog

And the cards catch the waves

Kingfish has to deal running rabbits

Concoct semi-bluffs

And shakedown a pair of kings

Just to stay close

But the full boats keep rolling in

It's Frank's big score

It continues through this night

And the next

At 7 Wednesday morning

Jennie shows with the kids ready for school

So after $1200 and handshake

From a puzzled Kingfish

Frank drives Tony back to Giant Burger

Comparing Wittgenstein's theory of private language

To Heisenberg's uncertainty principle

With the passion of extreme fatigue

Over a chocolate milkshake and fries

He gets a flash

He's got cash in his pocket

No dog

No wife

No dissertation

No Caridwen

Bench probation

Sergeant Tipton calling three times a week

He hates this New America

It's time to dust his heels

It's time to leave the States

Mustang Ranch

There will always be a few Singularities

That go through the Wall says Tony

As they head east of Reno

In their contract Jaguar sedan

But they're anomalies

Detached from historical process

Monads

Isolated from the reach of politics

And the pleasures of conversation

What counts is mass psychology

And the Singularities who stay

After almost fourteen billion years

The Will To Consciousness achieves self-regard

And becomes intensely afraid

Of everything it considers or contains

It can't bear the consequence of its victory

The significance of Knowing To Be

So it negates itself

Becomes The Will To UnConsciousness

What Freud called the longing of the animate

To become inanimate again

Oblivion

The rejection of thought

The insistence on superstition and habit

The Death Wish

But it's also backing up

Into your mother's womb

Backing up before your mother was born

It's Early Christians

Destroying Greek culture

And calling it Salvation

Medieval Christians

Torching neighbors for their property

And calling it Faith

Modern Christians

Turning sweet Day into military Night

And calling it Armageddon

But there's another Wall

Standing before total UnConsciousness

Again

A few Singularities find Enlightenment

Going through

Others

Like all-too-human bodhisattvas

Stay to help the masses

Recoiling from the brink of collective suicide

Our psyches rebound again

The Will To UnConsciousness reverses itself

Becomes the Will To SemiConsciousness

In the original tracks of Will To Consciousness

But now everything is wrong

Life is False

This Third Will is the Apparatus

Of the Nation State

The Church

The Corporation

It lusts for Global Control

It runs from Wall to Wall

Like a terrified rat in a maze

Like a standing wave of indeterminacy

Never achieving the Being of Consciousness

Or the Non-Being of UnConsciousness

The SemiConscious Apparatus

Is the institutionalization of Fear and Aggression

The Will To Power made Present

In the violent unmaking of Future and Past

Every day is the same day

Ripped from its roots

In Imagination and Memory

The SemiConscious Man

Has no independent existence

Outside this decadent Will To Power

He erases and rewrites his Identity

In submission to Third Will's chameleon demands

He's the Repetition Compulsion

Played out in self-deception and self-destruction

What we call the World is tragic audience

And unhappy proxy

To the self-annihilation of the Will To SemiConsciousness

In the SemiConscious Man

We can understand the excess of the Will To Consciousness

It's the nature of Life to exceed itself

And the Will To UnConsciousness makes perfect sense

Suffering is the impetus and articulation

Of all Philosophy

It suggests a therapeutic solution

Eliminate desire or desire the impossible

But the Will To SemiConsciousness is insane

A ghost

A vampire

A simulacrum

The SemiConscious Man

Can only experience his Existence

By annihilating the Existence of Others

The more Others he destroys

The more he Is

This is the secret of Will To Power

And why Nihilism deforms the Modern World

It's the operating system of the Apparatus

From the freemasons and illuminati

To the commercials on tv

The SemiConscious Man first rapes

And kills his children

His wife

His relations

His co-workers

And then turns to us

When the SemiConscious Man

Murders a Conscious Man

He finally

Totally

Is

He's the half-smart barbarian

Eating the beating hearts of Singularities

He's the predator

And we're his sickened prey

He's the scavenger

And we're his target carcass

The madness of the World

Is the vengeance of the SemiConscious Man

Eternally suspended between Being and Non-Being

A scalar wave of Hate

Building pressure and temperature

Until the World blows

If the Three Wills are in constant contest says Frank

Putting his fingertips together

Our Universe should be their accurate expression

Accelerating expansion

Could be a prime function of First Will

What physicists call dark energy

Is the finescale equivalent of Will To Consciousness

This is encouraging

Life wins out

However

What we see in New America

And the consolidating New World Order

Is the hegemony of Third Will

Over the First and Second

With the Apparatus in power

All human society is meaningless

Because it's necessarily False

We're forced to experience a New Medieval

Of cyberpriests and celebrity apes

That dehumanizes Life

And glorifies the ghoulish taste of the Undead

Schopenhauer's pessimism

Could hide in the museums of Art

In this New World Order

There's no psychological solace or escape

Art is Their favorite Torture

Torture is Their favorite Art

Yet Third Will can't rule

Without the massive complicity

Of First and Second Wills

How many Conscious Men and Women

Disguise themselves

As SemiConscious professionals

To cannibalize their conscience

And maximize profit

From the Terror of the Police State?

How many UnConscious Men and Women

Yield their Intelligence

To the SemiConscious Apparatus

And wear the rhinestone chains of New Age nonsense?

We achieve Conscious Society

When First Will unites with Second Will

To defeat the Third

The Living

Must restore the Dead and UnDead to Life!

Starting over means starting small

Means keeping the City Of Light

In the Measure of Man

We achieve Conscious Society

When we derail the globalist agenda

Of the Apparatus

When we dismantle the Nation State

Into independent City States

And allow Reality to regain its natural stream

We fight the New Medieval

With the Old Medieval

It's the core of the struggle

It's the hair of the dog

It's the singular dose

Conscious Society

Is the Future

Reaching back in time

To liberate the Present

Speaking of the City of Light says Tony

I think we're getting close to the ranch

Wait! says Frank

Why can't the Three Wills

Be quantum states of a single Will?

Why do these meta-events have to be linear?

If every person is a composite of three quantum states

Self-observation determines individual identity

You can affirm First Will in the World

By renaming it in yourself

You can affirm Second Will in the World

By reclaiming it in yourself

Observation is the quantum key agrees Tony

When I see the World operate this way

When I say what I see

It forces the World to choose

Either work my way

Or some other way

Of the many observers in the many Universes

I choose myself as the Prime Observer

I see myself seeing the Three Wills

I force the World to Be

The only thing that can change our Universe

Is a stronger observer

This is the job of Philosophy

This is the Will of Nietzsche's Uebermensch

I'm the Prime Observer of My World

And My Self

What's the theoretical alternative?

A hologram?

Nothingness?

But before Frank can respond

Tony spots the Mustang Ranch exit

And squeals the royal blue Jag

Down the offramp

Down a curvy gravel road

To a parking lot wound in red barbed wire

See the modest neon sign

See the white Bentley

In a dusty sea of Ford and Chevy pickups

They're through the security hall

Standing tense

As a green horseshoe assembles

They're all pretty

And it only takes a second

Tony wanders off with a freckled cowgirl

And Frank takes a busty Black with a fake ponytail

She's swaying friendly through the trailers

Where you from?

Chicago says Frank

Improvising

I'm Dominique

I'm from Chicago too she winks

Are you a musician?

Yes says Frank

Starting to get in the mood

You look like a musician says Dominique

My brother's the bass player for Hound Dog Taylor

That so? says Frank

Certain he's never had this conversation before

It's reserved for a man and his whore

When they get to her room they discuss her rates

Made reasonable

By the speed she's made him comfortable

Soaping his penis and balls over a pail of water

Dominique whistles a little Southside blues

And dries him off with a white terrycloth towel

This your first time ain't it?

What?

First time you're paying

Guess so

It hadn't occurred to him

Yes

Well that makes it special

Yes

She lays him on the polyester king bed

Takes off her robe

And poses her spectacular ebony body in blue light

It means double rates

What?

All virgins pay double rates

House rules

Frank's impressed by this new definition

And concentrating so hard not to come

That he readily agrees

What's another forty bucks?

After sucking and mounting him

Dominique changes her tone

You're no musician

I can tell by your fingers

Musicians have a lot of calluses

You're a liar

Her conversation's odd counterpoint

To the crescendo of the ride

You're on the wrong side of the Goddess Frank

You've lost your Muse

You'll never write anything of merit again

You'll wander the World and never know why

Like Odysseus you'll be Death's toy

A spinning top of Lies and cunning

Never knowing the reason you were allowed to live

Stop!

He comes anyway

And savors three minutes of silence

Dominique's wiping and crowing low

I'm the best

So answer me this

What is Truth?

What has four faces at dawn

Two at noon

Three at sunset

And one at midnight?

There ain't no whore where you going

That can read you like I do

Back home in New Orleans they call me Sphinx

And that's the way I want you to remember me

Dominique's no kind of name anyway

You gonna remember your Sphinx Frank?

When you defeat the hurricane winds of probability?

When you anchor in the cinnamon harbors of affection?

When Four plus Two plus Three

Is One?

You gonna remember my riddle?

You gonna remember me?

What riddle? says Frank

Dropping an extra fifty on the bed

He thinks he has it

But one wrong move and nothing looks right

He's underground

Underneath the trick palace of Minos

Bumping into prize fighters

Potbelly lawyers

Drunken minotaurs

Stopping to get a Coke from a rusty machine

Thinking of Lee Harvey Oswald

Stopping

To get a Coke from a rusty machine

Then back to the cowboy bar

Relaxing long-leg

On

The

Seafoam sofa

When Tony appears flushed

Asking for fresh cash

What's money for? says Frank

Watching the circus of clients arriving

The horseshoe forming and dissolving

The bourbon poured into the next galactic glass

As apricot anticipations rise from the east

Frank and Tony stagger out to the Jag

Dead broke

Slow sliding into black leather seats

Lovely girl says Tony

Definitely Second Will

How was yours?

A whore's a whore says Frank

Burning big rubber

As they retake I-80

A Flamingo Lagoon

After lifting a plastic bottle of Visine

From a Scarsdale convenience store

Frank and Tony really get the red out

And rediscover Superman's x-ray vision

They pile into Billy's racing Porsche 911

And hit the trotters in Yonkers

Trying to parlay this timely superpower

Into first-class tickets to London

The boys can see the winning silks

Before they flutter the finish line

They're packing their pockets with fifties

When one last drop brings the redeye back

Every trifecta goes south

Herve Villon loses his whip

And Billy's thumb has them slipping out

Through a flamingo lagoon of losing tickets

Before they go completely blind

The Highgate Rumba

There's a party in Highgate tonight says Tony

Over at Edwin's

The Earl of Anglesey

You can come in jeans

He's hip to the Left and Strange

And loves to flatter his high society girls

With articulate Communists

Mysterious spirits

And the cheek of dressing down

After a short walk through the leafy lanes

They show up around 10

Unwrapped by help in livery

And escorted downstairs to the séance

Whispering between black velvet curtains

We welcome two new observers

Announces Edwin

We welcome witness of the Beast!

Tony shields himself with polite irony

As Frank examines the writhing gray ectoplasm

Forming tubes and pyramids above the table

Master Aleistair reveal your desire!

Intones Edwin

Lifting his beefy arms to the smoke

As his guests concentrate

On a central foaming crystal ball

Why do you insist on juvenile pranks?

Retorts a sharp voice

Everybody expects the bald pate

The familiar sadistic glare

But floating above their heads

Is Lam

Crowley's Tibetan contact

Seething gray skin

And wraparound alien eyes

Release me this instant!

I have nothing to say to young fools!

They instinctively blink

And Lam disappears

In a blue snap of electricity

Well says Edwin

Stroking his bushy sideburns

It must be time for drinks!

Hey-ho!

They return to the reception hall

To mingle with newcomers

Spooning rounds of Stilton cheese

And spilling vintage champagne

On their posh buckled shoes

Edwin circulates

Introducing London's rich and clever heirs

To the Reds and Anarchists in The World News

Their carefully coiffed and pressed personalities

Brushing black motorcycle jackets

And flowing Arab gowns

If you see anybody

You're not supposed to know

It's because Guy Burgess

Made the invitations!

Jokes Edwin

Mixing

The Unbelievably Inane

With the Unconditioned Insane

Over Dom Perignon

Tony disappears into a connecting closet

With a brunette in lime pastels

And Frank allows a whiskey buzz

To take him towards the arboretum

Across an enormously immaculate lawn

And into a vertical grip

He's thinking trees are older

Trees are immeasurably older than Society

Trees are hardwired in our brains

Carried root

Sap

And leaf in our deepest personal mythologies

When he happens upon two lovers

Tastefully necking on a bench

Frank old boy!

Good to see you again!

Frank sees a look of welcome irritation

Wash the girl's face

As the man gives him a big embrace

It's Ilich

His Venezuelan friend from Moscow

Ilich with a jaunty new moustache

Still chasing expensive skirts

This one curses softly

And disappears

So they sit down on the bench

In a leftover cloud of Opium

To catch up

I went back to Caracas says Ilich

But ended up working for the wrong faction

And they threw me out

So we're both American Exiles now

Even if

It took you a bit longer to find London

English women are the best in the world

Well

Maybe not the best

But they love drugs and hold their liquor

So what more do you want?

Would you like Melinda's number?

Ilich leans close

You must tell me what happened to the Diggers!

Was it Hoover?

And the Weather Underground?

Breaking Tim Leary out of jail was High Art

Exceptional!

They're idiots

They're just SDS kids

Falling for their own press releases

They're retarded roadies

Who blew up the band by accident

So why are you here?

I resigned

I'm here with Tony

Maybe so Frank

But just the same

Powerful numbers in certain covert organizations

Think you're still operational

I'm in flight

I'm not fighting any more

Let's return to the party

I've got a better idea Frank

Follow me

Ilich gives him a swig

Of warm Swedish vodka

And they wander though dewy fields

Behind luxurious villas

To a small square cemetery shrouded in fog

Ilich hops the wrought-iron fence

And waltzes smoothly to the spot

Frank lights their Cuban cigars

With the exuberance of student conspiracy

They drink and smoke fast

Two bulky profiles

From North and South America

Sitting below the big black marble head

Of Karl Marx

After twenty minutes they're toasted

Praising each other in Russian slang

A little improvised soft shoe

On his ornate Victorian gravestone

Singing The International

And all the pub doggerel they can recall

Death To Capitalism! yells Ilich

Death To Capitalism! booms Frank

As they rumba hand to hip

Seven times

Around the only Philosopher

Who prized the World more than his own Ideas

They finally get dizzy

And fall to the wet grass laughing

One last salute to Health

Freedom

Fraternity

Then a sodden wobbling way

Back to Edwin's mansion

The butler gives them white terry bathrobes

To replace their muddy jeans and jackets

And these prove to be of great interest

To the bored birds lingering slim and witty

For the first erections of another Highgate party

The Three Names Of Lenin

From inside our frame of reference

We can see The News of the World

As a complex contest between agencies

Nothing is what it appears to be

And the message is always the same

If you don't obey the code in the text

We will kill you

Consider Bobby Fischer

They made him an American hero

For defeating Spassky at Reykjavik

The self-taught Jewish grandmaster

Defeats the atheist Russian chess machine

To become World Champion

But the map's not the territory

We know Fischer's a KGB asset

Irrational anti-Zionist

Easily manipulated

Spassky's the sophisticated Jew

Western sympathizer

Impossible to control

We know Moscow ordered Spassky to throw the match

Ordered Fischer to make outrageous demands

For his title defense with Karpov

So Their ambitious young Party apparatchik

Can become World Champion

Without playing a game

Spassky's retired from competition

And allowed to marry in Paris

Fischer's subtracted from The News Of The World

Hidden in a Pasadena Christian cult

And eventually allowed to wander

South America

Asia

And Central Europe

Like a bearded wraith

Like a fake Wandering Jew

Can you see the territory folding the map?

Another pint of Guinness? asks Ilich

Gesturing to a chubby blonde barmaid

In the Green Park Pub

The more you insist on your resignation

The more They think you're a Sleeper Frank

They assume you're programmed for something big

Here we go!

A toast to the News behind the News!

They clank and drink

I guess you know

I've been working for George Habash and Wadi Haddad

I shot the Zionist Joseph Sieff a few miles from here

And bombed two Jewish banks

Nothing important yet

Eventually I'll have my own network

But now I'm working with the Popular Front

The Palestinians are Exiles

In their own land

Denied both their Future

And their Past

The Russian Model is a Lie

It's not about the Workers

It's about the People

Castro understands the deeper Unities

The Russian Nation State

Is the American Nation State

They're both controlled by London banking cartels

And they both gave Israel the Bomb

So he promotes a barter economy

Free social programs for the Cuban People

Independence from the globalist bankers

The People are the Way!

Consider

They dismissed me from Patrice Lumumba

For attending an Arab demonstration

Why did they kick you out of Berkeley?

They didn't says Frank tense

It was my father

Yes

Of course

Sometimes I forget we're not the same Voice

Your father designed guidance circuits

For surface-to-air

And air-to-air missiles

During in the Vietnam War

He played golf

Maintained the yard

And took the family to the mountains

In a brown Dodge station wagon

He never explained his decisions

His mood was Law

He erupted without warning

I wish he were mine!

How easy to rebel

Against the dogma and domestic fascism

Of the Yankee middleclass!

A fistfight

How literary!

And you never went back

Extraordinary!

You probably saw him beating your mother

Or suspected it

You should be the one working for the Popular Front

Not me

My father was a rich lawyer in Caracas

Who overcame my theological tendencies

With a proper Leftist education in Cuba

He had a mistress for each season of the day

And Casanova's autograph in a safe

After Elba divorced him and took me away

He continued my Marxist training in Moscow

And encouraged my interest in languages

He still writes me twice a month

And always includes a substantial check

How can I kill such a father?

How could it even come to mind?

In the end

I'm sure he'll bring me to God

But you!

You denied your father and your God in one move

You just walked away

How fortunate

How free!

My father named his sons

The three names of Lenin

That was the limit of his lunacy

But your father thought genetic insanity

Would strike him down

While he was checking his oscilloscope

While he was watering the grass

While he was shopping at K-Mart

When he saw you

The Glendover curse clouded everything

Why were you so arrogant?

So vocal?

So indifferent to middleclass rewards?

Why did you reject his engineering?

Why did you resist his conditioning

Of Pleasure and Pain?

Of Presence and Absence?

Your father's perfect!

Made your life political

Mystical

Autobiographical!

Well

I'm going to Brussels and you're off to Milan

So allow me to propose a small wager

A bottle of good Russian vodka

For the first Fischer sighting

And a large tin of Beluga caviar

For the first Terrorist Star

I say the World's too small a stage

For both of us

And too large for one of us

We meet and then we meet again

You're on says Frank

With the odd and certain sensation

That his memories were being scrambled

To a slightly different frequency

And one last thing says Ilich

As they touch mugs to seal the bet

George gave me a new name

Finally something Spanish

I'm Carlos now

Letizia

Milan's a blur of High Fashion

Winking through scaffolding

Smog etched into pink marble palaces

Paulo lugging his Fiat to save gas

The hospitality of Riverside and Santa Cruz

Heavily accented by Milanese concerns

His jacket's too blue for spring

He should leave a bite on his plate

He needs a haircut to teach at Berlitz

Paolo's dating Rita

The slim daughter of the Jolly Tie empire

And one night after pizza in Brera

Frank meets her friend Letizia

She's a plump redhead with a Toto jaw

And gold-flecked emerald eyes

See her wrinkle her nose

See her light her Marlboro

He's staying at her lovenest near Piazza Cavour

Until she mentions warming up

With other men

So he gets a haircut

He finds Corso Porto Romano

He's learning the Berlitz Method

From a tall Prussian

Pretending to be a former Cambridge don

He's training with Angelika

A centerfold strawberry blonde from Munich

He's teaching English

For two dollars an hour

Napping between classes in a chapel

Then back addicted to Letizia

Walking cobblestone alleys to smoky lofts

Slipping past the doorman to a kinky penthouse

Never making it in the same place twice

He's tracing her facial scars with semen

He's living on cappuccino

Brioche

When Angelika invites him to lunch

And puts a monogrammed envelope on his plate

In his manic and thoughtless state

Everything's magnified

Mythic

He falls into her Big Bavarian Breasts

He falls into a Big Train Ticket to Heidelberg

He falls into a Big Escape from a Big Noose

Two Hours

Big black Mercedes 450 SEL

Stopped at a broken red light

3 in the morning

Thirty minutes

An hour

Two hours

He's lying in the grass drunk

With a trim dancer from the Cavern disco

The Rolling Stones

Sympathy For The Devil

Played on a loop

Thirty minutes

An hour

Two hours

Waiting for the World to change

The Logic Of German Girls

The logic of German girls seduces him

He sees Holderlin released

From his tall tower madness

Athena's domestic inventions sweetened

By the squeeze of Gothic thighs

The emotional manipulations

And financial targets of American girls

Happily forgotten in effervescent conversations

On European history and literature

They teach him German

With the simple grace of children teaching children

He's staying in Heidelberg forever

When he comes back from the canned food store

And finds Toby's letter on the floor

A Gentle Rocking Motion

Socrates was scared shitless of Exile says Toby

Wiping foam from his moustache

But we're doing well

A big flat on the Rhine

Two rich girlfriends

Teaching English for fifty bucks an hour

At Amerikahaus

Beating the ponies at Wiedenpesch

Meeting like this for cribbage

In the best breweries of the World

He was worried about Identity says Frank

Lighting a Dannemann cigarillo

He believed in Exile

You degenerate

Collapse into barbarian superstitions of Self

And socialized compromises of Virtue

Things are simultaneously too easy

And too hard

You lose the muscle and music

Of Self-examination

Since I left the States

I've lost that critical dimension

My identity's deflated

Lapsed into Frank Harris or Henry Miller

In Berkeley or the Haight

I changed characters a dozen times a day

And I always felt Dionysus

Rushing to meet me in the mirror

But Exile is Apollonian

I've lost the flexibility of my Destiny

I'm reduced to action at a distance

To the word American

But we're safe Frank

No cops

No agents

Plenty of girls and beer

Why can't we just dig it?

Aristotle would agree

Let America stew in its crimes

Let Nixon have his dirty tricks

We're out now

We're free

No says Frank

We're chained to the wind

Strapped to beds of ball lightning

And taken up in dark clouds of irrelevance

We're safe because They don't investigate

Or understand our deeper Intent

We're Tom Thumbs

Caricatures of our most accessible charms

Cartoons in a battered travel bag

Entertainers

I think of it like this says Toby

Taking a long draught

From Thales to Epicurus

The Greek Philosophers were looking for Truth

But after two centuries of complex speculation

They decided on Moderate Pleasure

Aristippus called it a gentle rocking motion

And I agree with the Cyrene

Germany's my gentle rocker Frank

I've been in Cologne over a year

And I've never had so much fun

Or respect in my life

After graduating from GTU

I knew I couldn't become a pastor

My God was Dead

Burned by Dessy

Buried in the Revolution

My father found a sabbatical position

Here at the University of Cologne

And I discovered classical homeopathy

Hahnemann tested every remedy on himself

So I started with Arnica

Frank?

What's going on?

Frank feels a sharp cramp in his bowels

He's going to crap in his pants

A chill attacks his heart

He's going blue in the face

A walrus waiter helps him outside

And holds his jaw

So Toby can put a sugar ball under his tongue

As the spasms subside

He remembers a sweet moment with Erin

And ten fifteen minutes later

He's watching the red trams clang by

Almost normal

What was that?

I don't know says Toby

We just treat the symptoms

The acute picture was Arsenicum

The remedy's more a vibration

Than a material dose

How do you feel?

OK

Good

We can finish the game

They return to their table

Order another round of kolsch

Shuffle

Cut

And play

Hard rocking the pegs around the board

Gertrude

Gertrude is Steffi's best friend

And they first meet in a Greek restaurant

So it's a modest surprise

After crashing a week in her studio

When Frank learns

She's the richest woman in Nordrhine-Westfalia

He knows about Wolfgang of course

He's the judo silver medalist

At the Mexico City Olympics

Who makes everything cool

To cover his major gambling debts

Gertrude owns Bushido

And three other dojos in town

At forty-three

She's imperiously fit

Cultured

Clever

Happy to be with Frank

And happier to be with his penis

She takes Polaroids of his morning erections

His afternoon and evening erections

Erections by the gold Japanese screens

Erections by the orange lava lamps

Erections by the Bodhidharma painting

Dating and arranging the shots

Like Warhol celebrities

In a brushed steel album

On her smoked glass coffee table

Often

Strolling through town

She'll forget Frank's there

Shwanzi we need to stop for some shoes

Shwanzi we need to transfer some funds

Shwanzi they have the tastiest Napoleons here

She buys the most expensive French cottons

For Shwanzi to sleep in

The most exotic oils for Shwanzi to bathe in

The most arousing lubricants to work in

It's bizarre

But certainly not unpleasant

And he has to confess

That without grass or acid

Shwanzi's in remarkably good form

Frank's staying at her country manor in Porz

When Gertrude pops the question

Shwanzi and I have decided

To take a little trip through southern France

And then around the World

Michelin two-star of course

Shwanzi and I adore simple food

Well

I was wondering

Would you like to join us?

The Piano

At a small country inn

Covered in ivy and ambivalence

Frank and Gertrude are dining on the patio

Complimenting the soft grassy air

And the predilection of Swiss cheese

To create continents in onion soup

When he spots a sharp blonde teenager

Peeking at them through her chatter

Later that night

As he shorthands Debussy on the piano

She steals up to him and asks in French

Are you an American gigolo?

Red Flag Day

The cabbie takes them to the wrong hotel in New Delhi

Gertrude wants the Intercontinental

But they end up across town

They're so tired

They check in anyway

Hoping for a quick nap

But Frank's restless

He needs a walk before dinner

He finds a trail in a fetid forest

Coming out near a small village

Surrounded by small fires burning the fields

He's walking down the center stretch

Watching old ladies prepare curry chicken

When something catches his ankle

A large gang of young boys

Wearing loincloths

Adidas

Puma

Sweatpants

Shouting curses

Frank's not concerned

Until a rock catches his shoulder

And another his right calf

His brisk walk turns into a jog

He's running for the original trail

But they cut him off quick

And he's crashing through the smoky fields

Shielding his eyes from the cinders

When a golf ball spins by his ear

The next one

Catches his right temple

And he's down

Transported back to The Wedge

In Newport Beach

Body surfing on Red Flag Day

With his buddies from Ramona High

He blows the tuck on a monster wave

And slams into the sand headfirst

He can see the Tunnel

He can see the Light

He can feel the gravity of the Pacific Ocean

Pulling him to the Other Side

But he rallies his Will

Stays Conscious

And stands up

Weaving in the spiky grass

He's OK

The gang's gone

So's his watch

India wasn't like this before

Something's changed

Maybe his expensive French clothes

Probably something else

He refuses to consider

Right now

Near The Tibetan Border

He doesn't know what lured him to Nepal

Until they visit the tankha museum

And buy three beauties from the curator

She says her sister's got one in a barn

Upriver

Classic blueskinned demons

And red dancing skulls

If he wants the old mandalas

Carried out by Buddhist monks

Her father's village is near the Tibetan border

So Frank persuades Gertrude to rent a jeep and driver

They're enjoying the show

Watching the sky open and close

Open and close

With calm regularity above the peaks

Until their rear axle breaks

They're boiling their water

Eating dried fruit

Discussing Goethe's critique of Shakespeare

When the driver splits

It's a slow slog uphill and down

Small ponds clotting the countryside

Filled with offal and the orange crust of disease

Gertrude's fifteen minutes ahead

When he falls on his face in the red dust

He's delirious

Breathing fire in the promised painting

Dancing on the major deceptions of the World

Around the Great Circle one more life

He's certain it's malaria or dysentery

Certain he's dying

When he hears Gertrude hire a runner

To get a doctor up from Katmandu

He loses fifteen pounds in two days

His flesh is falling off his bones

When a Big Moustache

Appears with penicillin

It's twelve days of glucose water

And contemplation

Sometimes you find Howlin' Wolf

And sometimes Howlin' Wolf finds you

He's watching a double rainbow frame the Himalayas

He's finally sitting up

He's finally Sitting On Top Of The World

Green Tea

On the plane to Bangkok

Frank decides Sphinx and Tony are both right

Second Will is cramping his style

He's hit the deck twice in the last month

It's time to get back to the high side of the road

So he vows to include Gertrude in his dreams

Say yes to the antique store

She wants him to run in Altstadt

He pours a small bottle of Hennessey cognac

And they're reminiscing about France

The time he choked on a snail

The cobalt windows of Chartres Cathedral

Things are clearly on track at the Bangkok Hilton

He's taking a shower

Getting loose

When Gertrude shouts through the steam

I'm going out to buy gold

I'll be back in exactly two hours

By then he's found

The World Championship of kick-boxing

In the sports section of the Bangkok Times

They take a chessboard taxi

And make the preliminary bouts

But Frank's unprepared for the folk orchestra

Setting up the rhythm of the punches

Or the smiley bookies prancing down the aisles

Taking cash bets

See one boxer in red

See one boxer in blue

That's all there is to it

The dissonant notes rising and falling to the blows

The favorite winning then losing to a lucky kick

The underdog winning then taking a dive

Frank loses seven fights in a row

Doubling up dumb with Gertrude's money

Tilting in Thai melancholy

He's forgotten about the antique store

And the World Tour

He's never had a losing streak like this before

Everything's riding on the eighth

And when he sighs down in his wicker chair

Gertrude's gone

She can't be appeased back in their room

She thinks he's a bad investment

He lied about being a good gambler

So he probably lied about everything else

His ticket's on the table

They're traveling separately now

Shwanzi you have an idiot for a master

Shwanzi remember to change your shorts

They breakfast politely

And board the plane to Hong Kong without fuss

They talk about fluctuations in the dollar

They talk about green tea

Too Much Nietzsche

He sleeps at the YMCA

And skips breakfast

Taking a train to the New Territories

On a hunch

He's walking through young shoots of rice

Towards a shack on the hill

Where he helped translate the Tenth Patriarch

When Master Yen appears

On the bright and narrow path

You've been reading too much Nietzsche

He admonishes with charm

As he takes Frank's arm

He's going to a meeting

Of The World Fellowship Of Buddhists

Mr Chou is ill

Can you assist this evening?

And Toronto?

That was your commission

You were the youngest disciple

To receive a transmission in the history of Chan

What happened?

I found the True God

The high strangeness of these words

Hangfire in the sharp rattling of the tracks

Until Frank finds his Voice again

He's Love

He's Bliss

He's total acceptance of Being

I found him in my personal experience

I found him in the hearts of mystics

From every spiritual tradition

He's an infant

Prescient

Precocious

And powerless

God is the World

Unable to distinguish

Out There

From In Here

Unable to move

Or speak with Intelligence

This flat expanding Universe

This object of our most passionate Intent

Is a defenseless baby

And our job is to bring him to Consciousness

Seen with Understanding

Every Emotion

Idea

And Act

Can only be authenticated

By doing this job well

Clever illusion Frank

You've traded the Enlightenment

Of the Diamond Sutra

For the cloak and horns of your vanity

This God is your literary mask

For all-too-common Desire

Yes!

I affirm this Desire!

I affirm this Life that wills its own Overcoming

I affirm this World that stretches Space and Time

To reproduce itself!

Such Singularity

Arising as low probability

In the indeterminate sweep of Time

And the luckless spin of sterile galaxies

Deserves to endure!

I affirm the tragedy of Consciousness

That circulates the bitter winds of personal loss

That crushes the fruit of its favorite creations

I affirm the bursts of human Singularity

That can defeat Death with a single joke!

I affirm the responsibilities

And ineffable joys

Of raising God

Only an idiot embraces Suffering

When he knows the way out says Yen

Your ignorance is the strongest evidence

Of your ingratitude

This God of yours is a literary conceit

A story you tell yourself

To cover the illusions you've diffused

After betraying the dharma

You sing with Orpheus

You sleep with Demeter

And eat the mushrooms of hallucination

You dance on the damp and dissembling stages of Hades

To rescue your implacable White Goddess

But this cavalier chess game with Death

Eventually loses humor Frank

You'll find your boots

In tracks made by madmen and fools

And you'll become these madmen and fools

You'll find your words

In the shrill taunts of hungry ghosts

In the howling chorus of inexplicable political events

And you'll become these hungry political events

Your Philosophy only sparks when you lose your Way

But what can you lose when there is no You?

Will is the most illustrious illusion of Desire

The most worthy adversary of Vigilance

Watch the Three Wills disappear Frank

Casually

Like clouds

Emptying a clear sky

Vigilance is Pure Consciousness

Pure Science

To choose any other Consciousness is perverse

If Enlightenment serves Death answers Frank

Then it's Second Will

And I want no part of it

If Enlightenment serves Life

Every moment is celebration of Future Life

And Here I Am

The Infant God

Is the solution of the Mystery

We must show God

How to reproduce his unique Information

How to fly his massive Electric Body

And find a loving Mate

We are older and wiser than God

Our job introduces him to First Will

So he can survive the inevitable attacks

Of Second and Third Wills

And achieve paternity

We are the Father of God

We are the Mother of God

We are the parents of the Universe

We must embody First Will

In every authentic Act

We must raise our children in Athenapolis

Or default to the vampires

Of the false Abrahamic God

Never knowing True or False

Being or Non-Being

Or the Love of our chosen descendents

Mark these words says Master Yen

Remember my face as I pull down this window

Approaching Kowloon

Because it will take a thousand

A million more incarnations

Before you understand the source of your Idea

And can let it go

Jack Parsons

Jack Parsons is my man

He knew Magick

Made him a great rocket scientist

Jack Parsons is my man

He could play both sides of Mind

Without bursting his brain

He knew the thing to steal from Crowley

Was the motto The Beast stole from Rabelais

Do What You Want Is The Whole Of The Law

The rest of Aleister is Victorian reversal

Sado-Masochism

Heroin

Eating menses and shit

In moronic rebellion to Society

I want a New Man

Springing from the clay of the Nation State

That castrates and enslaves him

So I create the Terrorist

Intimate and identical with World History

Indistinguishable from the Aristocrat

Jack Parsons is my man

I create the Terrorism of High Style

I am the New Man

I change causes with my Italian silk shirts

My network is comprised of high society girls

In the commercial capitals of Europe

They're my safe houses and escape routes

My salons and theaters

I teach them Jack's sexual Magick

And they become paragons of discretion

They become New Women

Intellectually alluring and politically astute

Gorgeous Athenas fighting the Apparatus in my name

My greatest success

Is my London lover

My Elba

My mother

Jack Parsons is my man

He invented solid rocket fuels in the morning

And interdimensional orgasms in the afternoon

Here was a Nietzschean!

The Russians wanted me to keep a log of my lovers

They demanded receipts for my whiskey

So when I left

I took the New Man with me

I created a cosmic file the KGB or Mossad

Could never find or fathom

I broke all their rules

I told my lovers the precise plan of attack

I gave them guns and fake passports

I gave them suitcases of cash

Jewels

They took nothing

They said nothing

They reciprocated my trust

With courage and keen anticipation

For the next set of instructions

My women are the erotic Body

Of New Consciousness

Jack Parson is my man

I transformed Terrorism into Magick

My little black book

Is the best political manifesto

The Palestinians will ever know

It's absurd

That's why it's great

Frank Glendover breaks through

When he understands

History is not what he believes

History is what They believe

If They believe in Good and Evil

Then we battle angels and demons

With the old Manichean swords

We defer our inheritance of Earth

Until Their Apocalypse is consummated

And the air is clean

As water

And the water

Clean as fire

Frank's my raging paradox

My elusive alter ego

I'm all Action and he's all Ideas

I can't stop thinking and he can't stop running

He won't acknowledge the whispered cue

He can't write a line

Not even a letter to his mother

Jack Parsons is my man

Here was a Nietzschean!

He knew that to make things clear

You have to make things happen

Man is the bridge to the Beyond

The Beyond is the bridge to Man

To the People

Morality is Terrorism

Terrorism is Morality

Action is the refutation of ethics

The utilitarian theater of Self-interest

That's why they love bad movies

Bad CEOs

Bad talking heads on The News Of The World

That's why they love SemiConscious propaganda

And its cynical pull on the nerves

When Evil calls itself Good

It confirms the People's deepest suspicions

Of themselves

And the real conditions of success

Consider

I bombed the offices of L'Aurore

L'Arche Minute and Maison de la Radio

I warned them by phone

That the devices were set to explode

At 2 in the morning

So there was major destruction

But no deaths

I sold the Good Terrorist to the papers

And cashed the check

By dropping a fragmentation bomb

In the acclaimed Deux-Margots Café

Bourgeois conversations had body parts

Swimming in their café au lait

See Carlos switch polarity

See Carlos the Evil Terrorist

Free Furuya of the Japanese Red Army

And force the French Government to capitulate

The tragic nature of my Being

Requires me to always be beyond Good and Evil

Always open to Comedy

With Rainer at the Orly airport

It was Keystone Kops

He misfired his bazooka twice

Missing the El Al plane and demolishing a hanger

The Japanese agents were gunned down

But my escape in the ambulance

Was pure science fiction

I'm a better escape artist than Houdini

I'm great because I create History

As you know

It's a rare and precious talent

Jack Parson is my man

My drama's for an audience of three

Wadi Haddad in Yemen

Omar Ghaddafi in Libya

And Frank Glendover

Stumbling somewhere in Asia

My favorite role is the playboy

With a weakness for small automatic weapons

When I was betrayed by Moukharbal

At 9 Rue Toullier

I came out of Paulette's bathroom

And shot the bastard in the neck

See Detective Harranz reaching

See his two policemen falling

See four bullets

Four necks

In less than seven seconds

Could Che Guevara shoot like this?

Could Che Guevara escape like this?

Could he run the rooftops

Following the phosphorescent arrows

Painted by his silk and lace?

Jack Parson is my man

I'm Magick

I can play both sides of everything

I can reverse the Fall of the World

With small automatic fire

Later that night I stayed with Analise

The young wife of the Paris Police Commissioner

We invoked the airs of John Dee

We smoked Afghani hash

And signed Jack's favorite sigil

With my pearly jism

And her steaming secretions

Pontoon

The rich young Aussies

Favor this hybrid of seven-card stud

And acey-deucey

Played stoned on rum and opium

With stout Balinese boys standing alert

To lift champions back into their chairs

So Frank comes to value pontoon

Charging like a desperate dying bull

Around the teak midnight table

He plays the small pots loud

The big pots quiet

Smiles at their gallows humor

And parlays his small stash

Into a good possibility of departure

A Small Gray

At Ubud they run cockfights

In specially vented barns

With a small gamalan band

And elementary girls taking bets

To fat fathers on the bloody dirt floor

Today Frank picks a small speckled gray

Against the giant Van Gogh beauty

Proud iridescent feathers

Green

Gold

And crimson

Attacking with a razor claw

Then suddenly dropping dead in the straw

The Infinite Surf

His young whore with twelve blue arms

Shows at midnight

Sucking the purple waves hard

For a dollar

It's simple diversion

A date with Shakti

In the infinite surf

A little Durga

To overcome the demons of the day

After a week he's bored

So Frank breaks it off

Thinking he's immune to Consequence

Until he hears a toothless hag

On the main road to Denpasar

Call his other name

And show five kids with open sores

Before Bali Rose Up Screaming

Island wisdom says

When you're caught in a rip go limp

And let it take you

To the coral reefs five miles out

Frank's body surfing the Indian Ocean

When the ninth wave goes flat

And he stupidly sprints for the beach

Cramps bouncing through his stomach muscles

Like pinballs of doom

There's no way to make it

So there's only one way to make it

With a simple release of finger and thumb

He drops his blue towel on the burning white sand

Before he went swimming

Before he woke up this morning

Before Bali rose up screaming from the ocean floor

The Spike

The first problem of Philosophy

Is distancing distance

While you're polishing a thought

You often run into something sharp

After a breakfast of black rice and bananas

Frank's walking the bluff

Working on Cosmic Acceleration as Art

When he sees his left foot sail clear

Landing safe on the trail

But it's also impaled

On a palm spike

And after two weeks of nausea

Amplified by the inability to swim

Frank finally allows the village shaman

To resolve the problem

With Japanese whiskey and a rusty razor blade

Astrid

To the hip international community

Of travelers at Kuta Beach

Astrid's a joke

Because she gives herself

To every guy leaving the next day

She's Swedish

Blonde and ingenuous

Nobody knows her game

Or unreported desire

So in his turn

Busy with late packing and goodbyes

Frank's intrigued

When Astrid shyly enters his hut

He's looking for a punchline

Something he once said well

When she reaches up through the thatches

And brings the Milky Way to bed

The Truth Rests In Turtles

After checking into the Raffles Hotel

He wants to see Singapore by rickshaw

Bouncing through the white paper lanterns

And sewer stench of the redlight zone

Until his runner stops dodging at a manor

Crouched inside a British colonial park

He's greeted with kind and professional smiles

Escorted to the parlor and offered unblended scotch

He's encouraged to paraphrase his taste

To match one of their International Girls

And soon finds himself in a tall window room

Talking Chinese with a student in pink negligee

She has the ivory luster of the classical Han

She's finishing up a small bowl of won ton soup

And the effect is so enchanting

He asks her opinion of the I Ching

And its Western translations after Legge

She feels his intellectual heat and continues to eat

Demurely closing her eyes to rising expectations

She says the Truth of the I Ching rests in turtles

The cracks in their backs reveal the cracks in ours

But her primary interest is William James

And they'd better get started

His Mandarin's flowing downhill

It's only been ten minutes

But he wants to pay for another hour

He suggests she refill her bowl

Watching her redefine the notion of motion

As she glides to the sideboard

But just as she turns to frame his gaze

Three goons burst in

Check the sheets for stains

Lift Frank up

And throw him through an open window

To the thick magnolia bushes below

The Thief

Frank investigates the night market

Haphazard stalls of junk

Lit with upstrung naked bulbs

Absolutely nothing of interest

Until he spots a young man in pajamas

Sitting beside a wooden crate

Cleaning a small vase with a toothbrush

Frank slides into conversation

On the geometries of Ching porcelain

And the five shades of Turkish blue

He buys the piece for $18

Impressed with the man's knowledge of kilns

And is about to move on

When the Thief says

Come back tomorrow night at the same time

I'll have something better

He does

And now as 11 approaches

Frank thrills to the prospect of treasure

But troubled

Because he knows it comes from graves

Of rich overseas Chinese

He can smell the lime

He can hear the bells of expensive Taoist spells

He wants to quit

But it's private access to a major museum

Right here on this wooden crate

He can hold classical Chinese Art

Buried for hundreds of years

He's bought twenty pieces

He's blown over a $1000

When the Thief says

Tomorrow night

I'll have a Ming

It's stupendous

A large demondog vase

Dragon design

Very Imperial

As Frank hands over $800 in fifties

The Thief's placid face wilts

He sweats

He ages

In

Slow

Ceremony

He turns the crate over and says

Now I'm the enemy of my Memory

Now I'm the enemy of my History

He wraps his eyes with a red bandana

And stumbles slow away

Only when Frank's back in his room

Admiring the porcelain on the bed

Does it finally compute

He's a fool

He's busted

In the City State

Where a parking ticket

Or a loud stereo

Gets you caned and three years in jail

What happens to an American Exile

With a roomful of forbidden graveyard goods

Who can't pay his hotel bill?

Pteripterix

He jokes with the bellboy in the lobby

Then walks down to the pawnshops

Hoping some miracle

Will turn his Hong Kong Rolex

Into cash

No chance

They just smirk

But he finds a $5 bill

Stuck in his passport

And decides to try the racetrack

It's a five-mile smogwalk

A dollar admission

He checks the Daily Racing Form

With some friendly Chinese students

And finds Pteripterix in the first

He's a big black colt

Named after the flying reptile

Broke down in his last race

But won at this distance nine months ago

Starting from the far outside post

Number twenty-two

Fifty-five to one

So Frank bets $4 to win

And climbs up to the covered balcony

To watch last money run

Pteripterix rushes to the lead

Clear by three lengths at the quarter pole

Clear by five coming to the stretch

It's the logical spot for him to quit

But he kicks out and wins by ten

Frank parlays his ticket into $2500

By hitting three later exactas

Buys German binoculars

For the friendly Chinese students

Loses a photo finish and cashes $1800

It's enough to pay the Raffles bill

And restore some cushion to his cranium

He's sitting at the Singapore Airport

Guarding two large soccer bags

Filled with antiques and newspaper

Thinking maybe the smell will give him away

Maybe he should just let everything go

He's edging to the adjacent waiting room

But his name still hangs big on the tags

And unattended baggage gets picked up fast

In the New World Order

He sees Port Security coming

Hears the boarding call

So he bluffs

Shouting and blustering about legroom

Until he's surrounded by nursing mothers and babies

Stowing the bags above a bulkhead seat

Thanking his new guardian angel

With the scales

Claws

And marvelous wingspan

Hit By A Thunderbolt

After five hours of flight

Frank falls asleep

And enters his recurring dream

He's curled on the metalmesh bed

When he's rousted

And taken to the visitor's room

His father's there

Wearing beige polyester slacks

And tennis shoes with cutout toes

Screaming diabetes

Something I forgot to tell you he says

Don't let them screw you in graduate school

After Caltech they promised me the moon at USC

But it was all Lies and departmental politics

I was furious

I took the Master's and left

Big mistake

Made everything harder

I wanted to teach

But the only thing I could find was San Bernardino State

And it wasn't enough to feed a growing family

So I went into electrical engineering

And ended up working for Howard Hughes

Stay the course son

Finish your Ph D

Dad?

Did you come to bail me out?

Did you ever call a lawyer?

Dad?

Are you even here?

And another thing he says

You could get a job at a gas station

You think it's demeaning

But a job like that can fix

What's wrong with you

It's not your fault

Trust me

Belief in something

And a normal job

Can help you transcend the problems

In our Glendover blood

Frank wakes spooked and shaking

Hit by a thunderbolt of personal alchemy

His father's a fake

The dream's a maneuver

He's really the twin brother of Ilich Sanchez

It's not about the Workers

It's not about the People

It's about the power to break with Fate

It's all about choosing the father you want

Crack

A bomb threat

Diverts the plane to Copenhagen

Frank's standing on the aluminum stairs

Freezing twenty below

Waiting for the Danish cartoon bus

In horizontal driving sleet

Holding two large Adidas bags

Close to body heat

When he hears something

Crack

At The British Museum

Well young man

Of the twenty-one Chinese pieces

You wished appraised

Twenty are attractive country works

Of peripheral interest

On the other hand

This shattered Ming demondog vase

Would be worth in excess of two million pounds

If intact

I've seen one other example in my thirty-year career

It's actual restored value I would place

At about five thousand pounds

And

Anticipating your question

To get it professionally done in Great Britain

Would easily cost eight

The Kensington Gardens

Athenapolis against the Apparatus says Tony

Walking a breezy June afternoon

Through the Kensington Gardens

It's the best way to value

The Modern World

Athenapolis is a branch

Of Individualistic Western Culture

Rooted in Athens

And the Florentine Renaissance

One Idea

One Experience

One Reality

Informs Conscious Society

The Individual becomes a Singularity

By enabling the Singularity of Others

It starts by guiding our children

And extends to every citizen of the City

Everyone masters the sciences of Mind

Everyone masters the arts of Body

To inspire the Singularity

Of future generations

In SemiConscious Society

The Individual is a statistical location

Of the Herd

From the Harvard professor

To the McDonald's line cook

Each location is a paranoid specialist

Programmed for obedience

Fear of losing Herd protection

And utter ignorance

The Apparatus is a virus from the East

Conquering the aristocratic West

With alien perceptions

Alien emotions

Alien thought forms

The first Abrahamic rule of Society

Was correct Vengeance

An eye for an eye and a tooth for a tooth

So the Law of the Apparatus

Became an eye for a tooth

The second Abrahamic rule of Society

Was love the Other as you love yourself

So the Law of the Apparatus

Became hate the Other as you hate yourself

These falsified Eastern rules

Became the Big Lie of the Apparatus

The propaganda

The babble

Of SemiConscious media

Every newspaper and magazine

Every radio program

Every film and tv show

Justifies it

In Athenapolis

The Individual becomes Conscious

In the free course of human events

Like a wave arrives on the shore

Or the wind bends the sequoias

When the Law makes perversions into institutions

Administered without check or balance

By the Executive Of Execution

When the Law attacks the noble tree

Of individualistic Western Culture

The course is no longer free

The Individual becomes an Outsider

A Terrorist

A Monster

More

In defense of personal Liberty

It's not about falsified Vengeance

It's not about falsified Love

It's about Singularity and Community

Athenapolis against the Apparatus

It's the best way to value

All Modern Philosophy

Well says Frank

As they find an empty bench

You have the utopian zeal of a confirmed misanthrope

But how do you think Singularity Theory

Can overcome SemiConscious control?

Where's your Athenapolis?

Floating somewhere in cyberspace?

How can you assume

The international banking octopus

And its Nation State satraps

Will allow you to survive your Idea?

Could Athenapolis simply be the name

Of your contempt for SemiConscious Man?

Of course says Tony

As they rise and resume walking

Without an understanding of the Three Wills

Life is a recurring dream

Dreamt by somebody else

Nietzsche called him The Last Man

Because he lives for his latest comfort

The Apparatus applauds slaves entertaining slaves

Richly rewards slaves killing slaves

It excites the sheep to act like wolves

It excites the lemmings to act like jackals

It excites components to unplug their competition

It exalts all the sick and degenerate passions

Yes

We must be discrete in our discourse

But we must also be bold

Athenapolis will survive the Apocalypse

In strategic chrysalis

Its first phase

Is a company of intellectual rights

When writers

Inventors

Other creatives

Contribute their royalties

To cover our initial economic needs

In the second phase

Emissaries of Athenapolis serve as peacemakers

For decaying Nation States at war

When we accept territory in exchange

For saving the World from military hegemonies

In the third phase

We secure energy independence

When our engineers install solar-powered islands

Producing electricity

Fresh water

Hydrogen for our developing City

In the fourth phase

Our scientists deploy advanced defense systems

Reverse-engineered

In Siberia and Nevada

Making Athenapolis impervious

To the nuclear

Biological

Conventional military attacks

Of the collapsing Apparatus

In its fifth phase

Athenapolis stimulates the birth

Of a thousand beautiful New Cities

And we achieve New Renaissance

We're not Winstanley

Content to raise pigs on St George's Hill

We demand the Fall of the Apparatus

We demand the Earth

In all its unfolding Mystery

Athenapolis is the Quantum City

That remains small

As it expands into Infinity

From a handful of astonishing Ideas

It's absurd

That's why it's great

Yes

Maybe you'll have to travel more

Suffer more

To understand these contradictions Frank

Oedipus was in Exile

Until he solved the riddle

Odysseus was in Exile

Until he understood his Way

Oedipus is Odysseus Frank

Everything Outside

Is Inside

The Mediterranean Sea

Is the fluid surrounding your brain

For all its humor and adventure

Your journey of Self-knowledge

Is a Tragedy

And the peaceful illumination

Of SemiConscious Society

Is a technical impossibility

That's why we fight

Why we demand Conscious Society

We start small

And we stay small

Self-sufficient and self-defined

We never exceed the Measure of Man

We never repeat the cancer of the Nation State

Or the corruption of the Global Corporation

We start small

And we become universal

Aristotle refused to follow Socrates

He mastered his Love and Hate of the State

He went beyond Exile

He transformed his Will To Consciousness

Into World History

Through Alexander

He brought his justice to decadent Athens

Through Alexander

He introduced his Philosophy

To the disconnected barbarian Myth

Through Alexander

He took a queen for each season of the day

Through Alexander

The World became Aristotelian!

Such magnificent Intent!

When the Apparatus falls

We'll need this expansive Intelligence

This natural Will To Power

Because the second problem of Philosophy

Is projecting projectors

Every Singularity imagines a World

Imagining him

Imagines a Cosmic Wife loving him

But while he's building the house

She stabs him in the back

She calls a lawyer

His hammer suddenly sounds hollow

She wants it all now

She wants what the other women have

She wants a SemiConscious Man

All conditioning is projection

All projection is conditioning

The SemiConscious Man

Is a hanging judge in the court of hypocrisy

He convicts Others of his own diseases

He convicts Others of his own atrocities

And substitutes their deaths

For each dying cell in his body

The SemiConscious Man

Is a concentration camp

Disguised as an amusement park

The SemiConscious Man

Is an executioner

In a business suit

And there's no finer SemiConscious Man

Than the SemiConscious Woman

She's the trusty

She's the informer

She's the sharp survivor

Who owes her place in SemiConscious Society

To the cynical political genius of the Apparatus

At the first sign of turbulence

She goes for the throat

The cash

The legal judgment

She liberates herself from her father

From her husband

From her lover

So she can work three male jobs

And give her babies to Moloch

The SemiConscious Woman is the backbone of Fascism

Let her go!

Her conformism destroys her Imagination

Her Virtue

And finally

Herself

Her babies are psychologically crippled orphans

Eschewed to the Nation State

Claimed as fertilizer by the Apparatus

You can thank the ancient instinct

That enabled you to leave Erin

That whispered to her

We Are At War

Consider

The Individual becomes a Singularity

By enabling the Singularity of Others

Athenapolis against the Apparatus

It's absurd

That's why it's great

It defeats the statistics of probability

It's impossible

That's why the SemiConscious Woman

Is the only road to Athenapolis

That's why Time

Is the place where three roads meet

The SemiConscious Woman is the Future

See her become Conscious

Like a wave arriving on the shore of her Body

See her become Conscious

Like the wind bending sequoias in her Mind

Next Time You're In New York

He finds a free ticket to New York

In Edwin's Chelsea flat

Circles JFK three hours in traffic

Then out to Westchester

And Billy's Scarsdale cottage

He catches up with Nixon's resignation

Emmett Grogan's overdose

On the last train to Brooklyn

Peter Berg's fantasy

Of yuppie urban ecology

They're playing nonstop gin on the patio

Drinking Tom Collins with a twist of lime

Billy's married now

He proposed after a weekend in Bimini

When they found Diane's dead cat

Stinking up the Murphy bed

She's a busty Ohio blonde

With a modern architectural talent

For erotic extortion

She carries kryptonite

In her Chanel purse

To deconstruct potential threats

From Billy's maverick friends

Her light conversation and bright hospitality

Anticipate poisoned compliments

With a pillow under her hips

Frank's slipping a confrontation

When he has a flash of counterplay

He calls Letizia in Milan

Invites her for a Grand Tour of the States

Maybe Mexico and Costa Rica

After gluing a bag of shards

Into the semblance of a demondog

He parks his Chinese antiques

With Rosenwald in White Plains

And smokes a Camel in the garden

Meditating on the strangeness of the trip

The unexpected texture of this American gate

Letizia shows in forty-eight hours

And Frank's ready to go

But now it's Billy and Letizia

Playing marathon gin

Smoking Marlboros and drinking sangria

She's got him by the balls

They play through the sticky Havana night

And pastel morning haze

Filling the wineglasses with fat ashes

And crushed plastic wrappers

When Billy finally gets even

He buys them tickets on the noon train

Adding Masonic

I love Diane

I'm happy teaching at Lehman College

I'm cutting out some characters she doesn't like

When you marry middle-class you'll understand

Next time you're in New York

Pass me by

O and Frank?

The girl can play

You'll keep track of the porcelain?

Of course

Good luck with Pokerface

And you?

I haven't written anything for years

I'm living too hard to write

So Billy's gone

They ramble to Philly playing cards

Thirty minutes of Central Station

Arguing about everything and nothing

Then hitching south

In a nasty afternoon drizzle

Thirteen Steps To Hell

In Northern Alabama

They lose I-65 near Athens

And get stranded at a Texaco station

On a bone-dry country road

Two good old boys with shaved heads

Say OK

They can climb into the king cab

OK

Just pass the bottles from the back

Ten cases of Pabst Blue Ribbon

OK

Turns out they were released yesterday

From a federal penitentiary in Louisiana

No Blue Ribbon in the pen OK

Did twelve years for assault and battery OK

Stole this truck across the line OK

Stole the Blue Ribbon here

The driver opens his denim shirt

And flexes his prison pectorals

Showing off a crude tattoo

A purple gallows pole

Erected above

Thirteen Steps To Hell

OK

Thirteen Steps

OK

After the second case of Pabst

They notice Letizia

Frank says OK

Pull over right here

The lady has to take a leak OK

They're posing behind a giant oak

OK

They're running crazy though the burn

OK

Underwater

In Monterey they rent a large room

And Letizia goes shopping for a whip

Mexico's very Catholic she says

They'll have what I need

They understand Devotion

They understand Surcease

Frank's more interested in a nap

And hears the good news underwater

When she climbs the creaky bed

It's Sixteenth Century she says

The knots and seven tails

Know me

Better than I know myself

Blues To The Moon

Somewhere on the dusty high desert

They stop for a Coke

At a cardboard bus station

On a nine-inch tv

Muhammad Ali and Joe Frazier

Pound each other senseless in Manila

It sounds like sundown blowing blues to the moon

But it's just a chord of vampire bats

Flying back from northern cattle ranches

La Paz

Mazatlan's a pleasant interlude

Eating fresh lobster

And drinking house tequila

But Letizia refuses to make love

And Frank's sullen all the way to La Paz

They find a shabby room

Attached to a peeling pink wing

They roll the dice

And Letizia wins

Seven

To

Zip

She undresses

And puts the whip in his hand

Presses her nipples

Against the stained stucco

And moans

Raking her ass with long red fingernails

Frank's speechless

Confused

Whip me Frank!

I confess my desire to you

Whip me Frank!

I confess to you

Whip me now!

Suddenly a complex neural discourse

That Frank thinks is Poetry

Fills the room with green noise

It's the Egyptian scarab

It's the form he's made of experience

The clash between intellectual affirmations

And the random unfolding of his life

Letizia's too real

Too close to categorize

He snaps the whip

And the scarab multiplies

Now it's a thousand green scarabs

Reflected in a thousand blue eyes

Letizia sighs

Cursing the absence of pain

What are you doing?

You idiot!

Do what you're supposed to do!

In crystal periphery

He sees Letizia massage her clitoris

Hears her orgasm

Groan staccato through the Wall

In dusty Burton melancholy

Frank drops the romantic story line

Picks up his travel bag

And escapes to that hard space

Where a man storms a squalid foreign alley

With nothing but distance on his mind

Prodigal Son

GTU receives Frank like the Prodigal Son

Gives him a sunny apartment on Benvenue

And a job at the library shelving books

The new department chairman

Accepts his radical theological study

Of Andy Warhol

As a dissertation topic

She suggests the AAR meeting in Los Angeles

T J J Altizer's the keynote speaker

So the Beverly Hilton

Room 210

Shortly after lunch

He declines a waterglass of Old Grand Dad

And they go straight into The Death Of God

After an hour Frank understands

The dialectical significance of Altizer's deception

He made the cover of Time

As the brilliant Southern Theologian who crossed

The Uebermensch with New Testament Gospel

He's tanned and fit

He looks like James Mason

He's a master of mirrors and sources

He's recruited Blake and Nietzsche as barkers

For his predetermined investigations

He tracks the original quote to Hegel

And now the Death of God

Is testimony to the Birth of Christ

It's the unification of Transcendence and Immanence

It's the Christological dogma of the Church

Recycled through its most radical critic

As Frank heads for the door

Altizer takes a rip and says

You're trying to do Theology without Faith

You're impossible Frank

Potentially Satanic

You'll find that all Philosophy

Presumes a Theological core

If I've made a saint of Nietzsche

It fulfills his prophecy

You're the alien in this house

You're the Morning Star

Their conversation spits

Rages

And spills into the evening seminar

Held in a biology lecture hall

Altizer's unshaven

Glaring in the French academic style

As Rubenstein revalues the Jewish Covenant

To include Christians and Moslems

All eyes are on T J J

As he takes a nip from a pocket flask

And replies with a mock critique of Derrida

Deconstructing Nietzsche's spurs

Inspired by Altizer's stylish deflection

Of Rubenstein's Idea

Frank stands to ask a question

And goes right into a rant

What you consider

Modern Christianity

Judaism

Islam

Are the surviving vessels

Of the Babylonian Mysteries

Devoted to Zero

You worship Nothing

You sacrifice your precious One

Your firstborn Son

Your Adam

Your Jesus

You sacrifice One

To Nothing

Your bloody Child Sacrifice

Is your fear and hatred of Life

Your bloody Child Sacrifice

Is your depraved social contract

With the Church and Nation State

You claim redemption of your sins

Through the grace of God

But this Stain

Ladies and gentlemen

Is permanent

This Stain

Ladies and gentlemen

Is You

Because you continue to worship Baal

In Jesus

Because you continue to worship Moloch

In Christ

If you had Tillich's Ultimate Concern

You'd affirm the bright bounty of Life

You'd affirm the physical and mental health

Of all future generations

But you understand no such Ultimate

You have no such Concern

You try to kill yourself by proxy

Destruction of the Other becomes your Christian practice

Torture of the Other becomes your Christian prayer

You have the virulent marks of Mammon

On every inch of your lizard skins

Theology as you practice it

Ladies and gentlemen

Substitutes the False for the True

Living Death for Life

Zero for One

And every natural number

Theology as you practice it

Ladies and gentlemen

Is both alibi and apology

For the unnatural power of Nihilism

It allows Marduk to command Los Angeles

It allows a moron to be President of the United States

It allows America to attack the World

It allows America to attack itself

Until New America is the official Memory

And the American Dream

Is the Universal Nightmare

For Theology to be real

Ladies and Gentlemen

It must destroy these Babylonian towers

It must protect and empower our children

It must make the Truth Human

And the Human True

Ladies and gentlemen

I ask you tonight

Where is your natural instinct?

Where is your Human Truth?

I say your Christian Faith is a Lie

A mask for World negation

And mass suicide

Ladies and gentlemen

My Ultimate Concern is healthy Man

What's yours?

My Ultimate Concern is healthy God

Ladies and gentlemen

What's yours?

God is the Infant Universe

Who needs our Guidance

Who needs our intelligent Will To Power

Ladies and gentlemen

God needs our Consciousness!

I ask you tonight

Who among you has the Will to defeat Zero?

Who among you will join me

In this great work of raising God?

Here

The distinguished professors on the panel erupt

Gasping and cursing

Satanist!

Gnostic!

Kabbalist!

Fool! shouts Altizer

Falling backwards off his chair

This is where you lose Eternity!

In tense moments of theater like this

The real danger usually comes from the audience

So Frank steps quickly to the speaker's table

As the students yell obscenities

And block the doors

Rubenstein's cool

Massaging the microphone

T J J Altizer has lost consciousness

And requires immediate medical attention

Would someone please call 911?

His ploy works

And when the emergency team arrives

Frank escapes

Carrying

The

Stretcher

He expects a chilly reception back at GTU

But rumors twist the facts

One report has Altizer wildly applauding

Another has Rubenstein agreeing in principle

With something Frank never said

He suddenly has national academic stature

His second comprehensives are pro forma

A glass of sherry and tangential conversation

With sympathetic UC professors

And Dean Welch

The only thing left is typing the dissertation

So he walks Sacramento to the Key Club

To celebrate with a few hands of poker

He's playing at the back table

When Jake The Rake appears on his right

Smoothing a thin new goatee

Letizia's at his elbow

With a cup of coffee

And a medium stack of chips

See her kiss Jake with maternal affection

See her take a long drag of his cigarette

See her flash her new wedding ring

Gardena

After swimming all night with electric dolphins

He's watching the tea steep

Hot to do it again

When Letizia yawns in from the bedroom

Trailing a yellow Chinese slip

It's just a thought he says

Something that popped up

In the kaleidoscope of possibilities

Tomorrow's Halloween

Let's go down to Gardena

And play a few hands

Sure she says

How much cash can you raise?

They hit Wells Fargo in the morning

A Persian buffet on Telegraph

Return for a romp in bed

And they're midnight at the airport

Waiting for the redeye to LA

He doesn't

Mention Jake

She doesn't

Mention Mexico

They take a taxi to the Rainbow Club

They're playing 5-10 draw

Touching each other

Mind to mind

The stacks of striped chips reflecting

Exciting new emotions

And accelerating new respect

They're using Sklansky's poker theory

To analyze key hands

They're in the Delmonico Motel

Throwing big fists of cash

At the blue tulip wallpaper

They win thirty-one nights in a row

They never get an apartment

They never open a bank account

They never get a car

They walk the Gardena streets

With wads of hundred dollar bills

Stuffed in their Justin cowboy boots

They bounce from motel to motel

Thinking of new ways to hypnotize fish

And play shills against the house

They can eat three dinners at once

Or

Nothing

For days

If the action is good

They're playing 10-20 draw

With sharks and drunken winners

They've come to know each other

Better than Man should know Woman

Or Woman Man

Frank can tell by the curl of her smoke

Across the room

If Letizia's bluffing

And she's instantly there

Massaging his neck and shoulders

After a bad beat

Halloween is Thanksgiving

Christmas

New Year's day

Easter

Now they're playing 2-4 lowball

At short morning tables

With the broken and botched

They're sleeping in the city park

Covering the pyramid

With blue plastic sheets

When Calvin

And another Korean pimp

Appear like turkey vultures on the slide

A couple of tricks can make a big difference honey

Couple of tricks

Big difference

Honey

Letizia's listening

So Frank buys a King George penny

At Gardena Coin And Gun

Fakes the flip

And they take the next redeye

Back to Berkeley

Over The Rim

They're crashing the Hilgard apartment

When a friend drops by with acid

And they trip to Tilden Park

The trails don't make sense

There's poison oak everywhere

They make love on a granite boulder

And come back scraped

Bruised

Thirsty for beer

Convinced LSD is dead

Frank has a hard time sleeping

He's woozy for two days

And then the sores come out

His face

His neck

His penis and balls

Are covered in itchy ooze

It's red

It's white

It's leaking where he scratches

It's swollen grotesque

He's hallucinating faces and places

As Letizia watches from a cane chair

Reading Cannery Row

Checking the bubbling lentil soup

I'm flying to Milan tomorrow she says

See a doctor if it gets worse

It's over

We're even now

Don't try to follow me

You'll be sorry

It's a week of rest and bootleg penicillin

Before Frank can think straight

His penis finally looks OK

He walks to the Northside Market

And steals a tin of smoked oysters

To speed his recovery

He's typing in the library

When he sees the White Goddess

In every woman reading

Every woman dreaming

And every woman

Is Letizia

He's hopelessly invaded

Totally

Possessed

Dr Welch is cordial

At their last meeting

Now that your doctorate's complete

You'll be receiving some intriguing offers soon

I'd like to see you here at GTU

But our policy requires a distance of three years

You might consider Hartford or Princeton

Altizer sent us a letter

Naming you the next great American theologian

If you can give up sleeping on floors

And chasing foreign skirts

I'll assist you to the best of my ability

In securing the academic post of your choice

Frank shakes the Dean's hand sincerely

But this isn't his Destiny

All Memory is volcanic says Frank

To a past Frank

It's not the country of his childhood

He hates this New America

They trashed the Constitution

And every defining amendment

They corrupted the Supreme Court

And every judge downstream

They installed electronic surveillance

In every brain and bedroom

They sold out America

To the brokers of Nihilism

And the American People don't care

Now he understands Aristotle

Sometimes flight

Is the most brilliant

The most efficient

Way to fight

Over the rim of his wineglass

Maybe Frank sees Letizia

Swinging down Le Conte Avenue

In a blue blouse and pleated white skirt

Maybe Frank prefers to live on the wind

He excuses himself from the conversation

On academic chairs

Lands at Milano Malpensa

And devotes the long bus ride

To details of the hunt

She once worked for a magazine

With an office near Piazza Repubblica

So he stands under green florist awnings

To catch her upcoming the metropolitana

It's the third day

A little after 5

Letizia's walking by

She's got a split lip and a shiner

She's got a new lover

A Florentine poet

No

She doesn't want an espresso

No

She doesn't want to play roulette in Venice

Caridwen!

I love you!

No

I told you not to come

I said you'd be sorry

Ulrike

In Exile

Every new city

Or any old city

Within range

Is another chance at romance

And reset

A chessboard wiped clean

Of the deciding blunder

A fresh-smelling harbor

After emotional shipwreck

Frank doesn't want to meet his replacement

By accident or design

So he takes the overnight

To Cologne

And applauds the German system

When his train arrives perfect

At 9

Toby's renting a room

From a classical homeopath

Specializing in Bach flower remedies

He's teaching English at Ford Europe

He's in charge of the TOEFL tests

At Amerikahaus

He's happy as a clam

They're playing cribbage

At the zoo cafeteria

Watching tugboats drag the Rhine

Steffi went back to her husband

Gertrude

Lost

Her

Fortune

In the Deutsche Bank crash

They torched Rosenwald in White Plains

Good to have you back Frank

It's probably all for the best

There's a party tonight at Jurgen's

They stroll downtown with their instruments

Play a few tunes on the Schildergasse

Toby banging his old Martin guitar

Frank playing everything in C

On his Hohner blues harp

They pick up a hundred marks

And give them to the gypsies

Huddled baby blankets on the stoops

It's German hip

Pretzels and dip

Refrigerator full of kolsch

Schnapps

People winding up the ornate stairs

Drifting through the tidy rooms

Ulrike's there with Hans

A German radical living in Belfast

Telling convoluted stories of the IRA

She works at DeutscheWelle

She knows the US Information Agency

She's a mole for the Baader-Meinhof gang

Her apartment overlooks a train-switching yard

Her vagina smells of freshly mown grass

Sometimes vanilla

Sometimes a hint of apricot

Frank's helping with the tests

Lecturing on Jimmy Carter

And The American Dream

At German academic high schools

They lunch with the Amerikahaus staff

Mining information on the soft spies

At the Voice Of America

They cruise Cologne

Taking pictures of old gumball machines

Bolted to forgotten alley walls

A few from the Weimar Republic

Twenty Nazis from the Thirties

Ulrike works overtime at the radio station

To polish her chromium cover

Frank picks up private English lessons

From politicians and business executives in Bonn

He's teaching the President of the German Industrial Union

How to tell American jokes

For an international symposium in Chicago

He's advising exchange students on American universities

He's got his Ford executives hooked

On a soccer pool

The week's winner has to find

A prodigious bottle of unblended Scotch

Or Kentucky bourbon

To share with the next English class

Frank's in a groove

It's hot and easy with Ulrike

Coming in her wonderland of scents

She's got a raven Parisian bob

She's a long-distance runner

She digs Bob Marley

And best of all

She brings him luck

He feels taller

Faster

Stronger

He wins a contest in Stern

For a Seiko wristwatch

And twenty minutes of tennis

With Bjorn Borg in Dusseldorf

When Carnival takes Cologne

And lipstick Huns flood the streets

Frank goes happily to ground

Securing a short case of Rhinehessen wine

A stick of Afghani hash

And enough canvas and oils

To paint sixteen versions of Ulrike

Undressing in the dark

The Job

The third problem of Philosophy

Is dialing dialectics says Dessy

Slapping his passport on the table

The methodology is sterile

Because you can never come to the point

Where your present question is clearly better

Than the previous

Or any answer less evasive than the next

Your friend Tony

Dialed up a new system based on Will

That appeared to be a flower of that same Will

But it had nothing to do with dialectics

It evaded Philosophy

By calling itself Philosophy

Which brings me to the question Frank

What am I going to say next?

He shakes his head

He knows

But he wants to hear it

From her

Our intelligence indicates that Ilich Sanchez

Has now earned the trust of Wadi Hadad

He's been given $5 Million

And orders to organize

A major new terrorist attack

Your job

Is to kill Carlos

I'm your Company contact

You know this

You've known this for a long time

Probably when you left Berkeley

Surely since you met Ulrike

We need to get to Sanchez fast

He'll never suspect you

Always has says Frank

Even so

He thinks you won't pull the trigger

We know Ulrike's in the Baader gang

We can pick her up any time

The code in the text is unmistakable

He knows this button nose

This lustrous Brown Cuban skin

She's out of uniform

Wearing an attractive cream suit

A frilly white blouse

A gold necklace of Black Stars

Or would you rather have Letizia back?

Everything's possible

You know how we create History

We can go either way

We can embellish your Life

Or accelerate your Death

You are the Job now Frank

You have no Will

You've never had Will

You're not in Exile

You've never been in Exile

You've been watched and healed

Every step of the way

The doctor in Nepal

The shaman in Bali

Tony

Toby

Paulo

Angelika

Gertrude

Letizia

Billy

Dr Welch

They've all been working for us Frank

Keeping you alive

Keeping you healthy

Asleep

Available

And now we're calling in our marker

We have to eliminate Carlos The Jackal

Before he blows up the Free World

You're our Sleeper

You're our MK Ultra Man

You have no Will

You've never had Will

You're my secret lover

So here

Dial your passport

No more dialectics

Ilich Sanchez is in Milan

Teaching Russian at Berlitz

Dial your ticket

First class cabin

O

And here's your gun

She hands him a black leather shaving kit

With a distinctive bulge

Frank's got one foot on the spiral staircase

One hand on the rail

Dessy's brushing invisible crumbs

Off her jacket lapels

With squared pink fingernails

O

Frank

When it's over

When you know what we mean to each other

What we've always meant to each other

Could you visit me in San Francisco?

My key's in the kit

My new address is 23 Goose Hollow Lane

Remember Frank

I'm the only one who doesn't betray you

23 Goose Hollow Lane

My key's in the kit

Modern Man

I'm the New Man

The New Man is mine

Modern Man has proven himself venal

Sly and incompetent

Resentful

Still keen

To pose in the Red King's clothes

And ride the Red King's mistresses

Modern Man

Is a statistical ape

A mean worm

A shuffling herd of obscenities

Feeding on envy

Greed

And gilt ephemera

Modern Man prefers his cubicle

His castrated vocation

His fast food and narcotic prescriptions

His manic shopper wife

Whenever he's stepped on

He doubles up

And calls the jackboot God

Yes

Modern Man doubles everything up

And calls the jackboot God

Everything's exaggerated

Everything's hyperbole

Violence

And The News Of The World

The Last Man's a small man

Smaller than the ants

Harry Lime spied

From the top of the Ferris wheel

The Last Man reduces Life and Death

To worn sofas

Wheezing in the boarding house

Of vicarious experience

Always crying out for something better

Always choosing something worse

I'm the New Man

The New Man is mine

I'm the new John Baptist

Dunking believers in rivers of bloody Consciousness

Turning every man and woman into a Terrorist

By building the bridge to Future Man

There are still some who claim

Anarchism works when it provokes oppression

They think it sparks Revolution

Nonsense!

Disinformation

Worse!

The Apparatus can always turn another screw

SemiConscious Society is the nemesis of the Individual

What we prize as Western Culture

Is the eluding

The outrunning

The overcoming of sick Society

Modern Man and the Apparatus

Are perfect together

They stroke each other

They deserve each other

I create Terror as Art

To destroy this diabolical union

Frank's a dreamer if he thinks Singularities

Will compromise their survival

To enable the Singularity of Others

No wonder he can't write!

He still doesn't comprehend the flush

Of Modern Times

I was a happy child in Caracas

A carousing student in Moscow

I've met the Rothschilds in London

I've met Nixon and Brezhnev

I know the Apparatus is deranged

Our species is dying

Our course is written in the stars

Every sixty-three million years

Ninety per cent of all species die

We're at least two million years overdue

We're already dead

This is the primary assumption of Third Will

This is what the Apparatus is saying

In every ad and press release

You're already dead

So it doesn't matter

Give us your money

Give us your vote

Give us your body

You're already dead

So it doesn't matter

I'm the Revolution

The Revolution is mine

I overturn the Covenant

No tribe is chosen

No tribe is saved

This heinous Eastern belief

Has crippled rational Western Culture

It's all about Art

All about Aristocracy

The Transcendent Gesture

The Literary Conceit

The Noble Death

Terrorism is the Conscious Action

That authenticates Modern Life

My pity for Modern Man has leaked out

Through the rhinoceros skin of the Universe

Modern Man is a mistake!

My Life means nothing

My Death means everything

I'll die like an Apache

Like a Celtic King

Like the last singer of the Bock saga

Sure

The SemiConscious Apparatus

Will try to erase me

Toss me in the Memory Hole

The Apparatus will insist

You sprang directly from the greasy thighs

Of the Nation State

That you came from Nothing

That you work your Life to the bone

And return to Nothing

It will force you to into zombie cubicles

It will force you to forget all Affection

Renounce your mother's breast

The Apparatus is a machine

Programmed for annexation and sterilization

What do I have in common with these robots?

These Last Men?

Nothing!

I love my parents

I love them in everything I do

This is my Enlightenment

It's reserved for the Few

Every breath I take

Is a symphony of filial piety

The Confucian Chinese

Know what I'm saying

My ancestors are my descendents

My descendents are my ancestors

Terrorism is my public service

I'm a Star of military history

I defeat the Oppressor

With the sword of Self-knowledge

I restore Man to his Free Domain

In a moment of weakness

Nietzsche called me the Blonde Beast

In a moment of great penetration

He said turn everything that's happened

Into something you willed

Amor Fati!

This

Is my Spirituality

If it happens

I willed it so

Will is the Whole of the Law

Yes!

I affirm Everything

Every time

All the time

I'm the New Man

The New Man is mine

No matter how you condition

And recondition Modern Man

He's still an eyesore

A greedy ox

An artificial intelligence

Too dumb to moderate his pleasure

In the pain and suffering of Others

I'm the New Man

The New Man is mine

I'm the apocalyptic wind

Bringing World Destruction

And World Rebirth

I'm the first green blade of grass

Punching up through the radioactive ruins

Of the SemiConscious Apparatus

I'm the first Star

Of the first constellation

After the end of Time

I'm Che's New Socialist Man

The World is my overflowing

I'm the New Renaissance Man

And everything comes to a close with me

I burst

I dissolve into the free geometry of the Future

I inform and levitate the Universe!

What's gravity to me?

Who's this Last Man?

This SemiConscious Man?

This Modern Man?

This ridiculous maggot!

He gives up his Being

For infantile avarice

He mortgages his Identity

For harpies and hokum

The World shakes him off!

I'm the Prophet of Authenticity

I'm Magick

The only authentic act is Art

Man is my canvas

Terrorism is my bridge

I'm the Uebermensch

The Uebermensch is mine

I continue what Nietzsche began

I'm beyond Good and Evil

I'm the Distance

That times Time

And the Time

That distances Distance

I'm Magick

And I despise Modern Man

The Vienna Raid

The History Of The Western World clearly shows

That when you want something done right

You pay a German to do it

So

With Haddad's Popular Front money

I went to Frankfurt and recruited survivors

Of the Baader-Meinhof gang

Wilfred

Joachim

Gabrielle

Became my operational team

For the raid on OPEC headquarters

In Vienna

Our History also discloses

Revolutions are planned in breweries

And cold mountain caves

So to put my monogram on these things

I invite my three Germans

Two Palestinians

One Lebanese

To the Vienna Hilton

And rent the entire seventh floor

With my new goatee

And faded black beret

I'm a bigger Che Guevara

I dress my team in disco outfits

Clashing colors and bellbottom pants

We dine in Vienna's best restaurants

Analyzing plans over veal schnitzel and champagne

The bourgeoisie thinks we're a theatrical troupe

Rehearsing a Greek tragedy

Our tips are monumental

So the management is discrete

Our detailed discussion of the raid

Proves to our fellow diners

We're following an ancient script

And Saturday night after dessert

We take a brief bow

To a polite round of applause

Sunday

I'm first into the OPEC building

Gabrielle kills a guard

I kill a fool

And formally announce myself

To the OPEC ministers

As The Arm Of The Arab Revolution

Working with the Popular Front

I'm Carlos!

You know me!

I put them into three groups

Liberals

Criminals

Neutrals

Haddad was specific

Only Sheik Yamani of Saudi Arabia

And Iran's Amouszega must die

Everybody else was negotiable

We wire the oil ministers to bombs

And demand Austrian national radio

Broadcast our communiqué

Every two hours

Or we detonate the hostages

Taped to the skyscraper windows

My first statement was in English

I wrote a longer one in French

Explaining the grievances of the Palestinian People

I spoke formally with the ministers in Arabic

I joked in Russian

Spanish

German

And every other mother tongue in the room

This was the apotheosis

Of a lifetime of language lessons

Begun as a boy in Caracas

Could Che converse like this?

Could Che joke like this?

While we negotiate for the DC-9

I put a loaded pistol on the table

Planting the seed of heroic action

In the arrogant pants

Of these Last Men

Freezing them in their impotence

Next morning I pose by the bus

Defying the snipers

Embracing the released OPEC employees

As the hostages board the plane

Otto Roesch

The Austrian Interior Minister

Walks briskly through the fresh snow

To shake my televised hand

Here's a man who appreciates High Art!

I'm relaxed during the flight to Algiers

Drinking Perrier water

Sucking on limes

Walking the aisle

Signing autographs

Yes!

The hostages understand the value

Of my signature

Moamar Ghaddafi gives me $10 Million

For the Vienna raid

And $1 Million a year for life

So we play a little charade

For the News Of The World

I fly from Algiers to Tripoli

Moamar refuses permission to land

And I'm back in Algiers

Four days sleepless

Negotiating with the big Arab players

I finally release the hostages for $60 Million

Paid in gold bullion by Saudi Arabia

Through the usual intermediaries

My drama's finished

I'm the Most Famous Man in the World

It confirms the vows

Frank and I

Made in Highgate

It's the best death of Capitalism

The most expensive

The most theatrical

Best death

Let Modern Man squeeze his paycheck

And idolize his Nation State

I can make $60 Million in five days

And prove that Revolution pays

When Haddad calls me to Yemen

To analyze the action in Vienna

Gabrielle and Joachim say it's my fault

Yamani and Amouzega survived

So after a brief call to Saddam Hussein

I agree

To me

The bastards

Were far more valuable alive

Stars are very bad at following instructions says Wadi

There's no room for Stars in my operational team

You

Can

Go

Lucky In Milan

Frank's lucky back in Milan

He retrieves his King George penny

From a granite gargoyle

Defending the golden Madonna

High on Duomo

And finds his lost book of numbers

Under a stack of fashion magazines

In Paulo's attic

It's hot and muggy Piazza Corvetto

The night air heavy with the orangeflower scent

Of condoms and syringes

Hard

To

Sleep

Awakened by jackhammers

And a mosquito bite

On his right thumb

He's chasing a fat buzz

From corner to corner

With a pink Gazzetta Dello Sport

When the phone rings

It's Ilich

Ready for La Spezia?

What?

We've entered the Torneo Magistrale

Could get interesting

Five Yugoslav grandmasters

Three Russians

A Dane

We're playing in the Duke's parlor

Late Eighteenth Century

Wonderful wood inlays

Are you at Berlitz?

I'll pick you up in twenty minutes

Have you seen Ulrike?

Consider Frank

My white Mercedes 450 SL

Is the new image

Introducing the final frames

O

And Frank?

Yes?

Bring your shaving kit

We won't

Be coming back

Jose Altagracia Ramirez Navas

This story was written by Calvino says Ilich

Smiling sideways at Frank

As they cruise the Autostrada del Sol

We're driving with the top down

And get stuck in a traffic jam

There's an assassin following us

In a silver Porsche 911

No matter how many lanes we change

Now matter how fast or slow we go

The assassin stays perfectly on our tail

And when things grind to a halt

I kill him

Before he kills us

That's not how it goes says Frank

He's not

Who we think he is

It doesn't matter

We're also fictions

Everything's Eternal Recurrence

We repeat every event infinitely

But each time it's different

We're different

Identity is this difference between

Our perceptions and our recall

I see brake lights ahead says Frank

It's not a job continues Ilich

It's Necessity

In this shattering second

I must act

Or I'll never be able to act again

The traffic's slowing

Can you see the Porsche?

Frank checks the side mirror

And turns

Maybe

The assassin takes many forms

Moro was murdered by CIA agents

Shapeshifting as supermodels

On Kissinger's arm

The Porsche is

And is not a Porsche

Right lane

Twenty cars back

Yes

Frank spots it

They're decelerating

Stopping

A Fellini wave invades the scene

Teenagers with painted faces wipe the windshield

Crones with canes sell blood oranges

Frank looks closer at Ilich

No moustache

No beret

Shaved head

Deep tan

Aviator sunglasses

The dichotomies and ideologies

Of Communist-Capitalist

Russian-American

Moslem-Jew

Resolved by the mad sting of Memory

He's become what he is

An entrepreneur from Damascus

Selling his black political solutions

To the highest bidder

Give me the gun!

What?

Your gun!

Frank reaches into his kit

And hands it over

I do this for us

I do this for the World

I repeat this

To transcend Repetition Compulsion

Ilich swings out of the driver's seat

Crouches at the fenderwell

And stalks bronze back to his prey

In the rearview mirror

Frank sees Dessy sitting with Tony

In a blue BMW sedan

Left lane

Fourteen cars back

She's speaking into her lapel pin

Now the Porsche

Instantly switches lanes

Five cars back

An old man with thin white hair

Fiddles with something in his lap

Ilich looms

And shoots him in the neck

The horn sticks

A hundred horns

Stick

It's Italy

The traffic's starting to move

The BMW disappears

It's done says Ilich

Handing back the gun

Again

It's done

Now we're Brothers

Now everything's a possibility

He was loading destroyer bullets

It only takes a scratch

This is the place where three stories meet

Your Exile is over Frank

You can return to the States

Who was he? asks Frank

Touching his fingertips

Jose Altagracia Ramirez Navas

My father

My dreams should be better now

And so should yours

Necessity makes the UnConscious Conscious

We take an accident from Sophocles

And make it ours

Conscious Patricide is our first Freedom

The common ground of Revolution

The cure of choice for an Apparatus

Running on the blood of infanticide

What I've done here today

Restores the World

Again

What I've done here today

Recovers the myth of Self

Again

We're on our way to La Spezia

We enter a traffic jam

We remember a Calvino story

And the rest is Magick

I always thought my father

Would bring me to God

As Cocteau said in Orpheus

Art must astound the artist

The sophistication of its Vengeance

Transforms the emptiness

And soothes the absurdity

Of a creation's Self-consciousness

We're all beguiled believers

Before we find our Will

My father cannot be the assassin

Yet he is

He was loading a gun

With destroyers

Identical to yours

It only takes a scratch

My father cannot be God

Yet he is

It was him or us

You looked back

And your Cosmic Wife was lost

You looked back

And found the Three Wills

The Nightmare ends

Again

My dreams should be better now

And so should yours

Seen from this height

Every authentic act is Patricide

Every Life preparation for a Noble Death

Jose Altagracia Sanchez Navas was God

His immortality is guaranteed

As long as actors read

And readers act

I killed God

Because he was blocking my way

I killed God

Because God is Dead

The Marks

Signor Attori holds the cards aloft

Like samples of precious vellum

Announcing the pairings at La Spezia

In silky patrician tones

Swirling against the rosewood panels

Ilich has Janovic with white

Frank Taruffi with black

They're researching the Najdorf Variation

Of the Sicilian Defense

Preparing novelties for the first round

They're walking down by the pier

Speculating on the original

French sense

Of Brotherhood

When they come to a white villa

Tucked under a crumbling cliff

Lunch is risotto with saffron

Dolcetto to wash it down

I see your dancing eyes Frank

We won't be playing chess this afternoon

Your head's boiling with Invention

Your cherished Caridwen

Is back at your side

The Glendover curse is lifted

We outran and outlasted the storm

Now your Exile is over

You can write again

This villa is a legendary brothel

Mentioned by Petronius

Notice the nautical murals

The Sabine knot decor

Mama Udoni takes you upstairs

Her massive shoulders and pendulous breasts

Excite the ancient mysteries

She introduces you to The Sailor's Friend

It slips on your penis like a Chinese finger puzzle

She pulls the strings until your glans

Is a burgundy boxing glove

And you punch for two hours straight

She straddles you

Singing Old Irish chanteys

Until you black out

The marks of The Friend

Never leave

Your Memory is that glove

Your Memory has always been that glove

You were flying over and under the World

But now the World presses in

Your Mind and Body are closer now

You're vulnerable

Susceptible

You can entertain your fantasies

And your fantasies can entertain you

You can bring Ulrike down from Cologne

To wear her white silk top

Tight black jeans

And Adidas tennis shoes

She's hungry for penne arrabbiata

And sterling conversation

You're holding hands under the table

At a two-star locanda on the Po

You're parked close to the river

Talking of the radio broadcasts of Ezra Pound

The American hostages in Tehran

When she dons a Frank mask

And you masturbate together in the car

To a chorus of sarcastic bullfrogs

Next morning brushing your teeth

You see her fingerprints

Burned

Into

Your

Palm

These alluring dark swirls

Also never leave

You can write again

The White Goddess deceives you again

I deceive you again

As we approach the end of the trip

The trip begins

Next stop

The Mountains Of The Moon

The New Babalon Working

Athena was born on the coast

And a thousand miles east in Cairo

Crowley received the Book of the Law

From Aiwass

These winedark Libyan dunes

Are the Mountains of the Moon

And if you can resolve this enigma

Many things become clear

Do you have your book of numbers?

Your gun?

Tonight we change the World!

Tonight you're my Scribe

For a New Babalon Working

Tonight you're Ron Hubbard

You've got the red hair

The flair for science fiction

Singularities learn best

From the mistakes of Singularities

Sometimes a great performance

Only requires a superficial resemblance

Jack wanted to accelerate the Age of Horus

He cobbled together some John Dee

Some Crowley

And flew straight into disaster

Jack lost his Way in wishful thinking

In poor character judgment

But his biggest mistake

Was craving Company

It frustrates the esoteric flow of Magick

It fouls the instincts of the Lone Wolf

By calling an Elemental

To be his Cosmic Wife

Jack induced the Other Side

To ravage his Life

It starts with Ron stealing Betty

Subverting the Pasadena invocations

Faking the Mohave Desert epiphany

Then running off to Florida with the girl

With Jack's fortune

Yes

Cameron's a pretty picture

A relentless artist with crimson hair

And eyes that change color with polymorphous Desire

But she only knows her lines

Her positions

She's fascinating

But infertile

Jack's sparkling Company

Exploits him emotionally

Financially

Magickly

Betty marries a New York banker

Ron founds Scientology

Cameron plays Kali

In a cult film for Anger

And ends up a backseat witch

For the California Hell's Angels

When Jack loses his top security clearance

He's back making cheap explosives for hire

The delicate link between sorcerer and scientist

Snaps in his futile wish to resurrect Affection

He changes his name to Belarion The Antichrist

Writes imitation Crowley trash

Films himself making love

To his mother

Here's a Sanchezian!

Jack Parsons is my man!

After a stint charming bullfighters

And their slender daughters in San Miguel

Cameron returns to the stage as Jack's wife

Waiting breathlessly

Film noir

In the car

When his garage lab explodes

The News Of The World says accident

Fulminate of mercury

But we know it's assassination

We know it's certain covert organizations

Connected to the CIA and Howard Hughes

After a languid Mexican vacation

Jack was headed to Israel

And a fresh start

Selling rocket fuels to The Eastern World

His mother commits suicide

When she's told

All evidence says the Babalon Working

Was a failure

But as Kenneth Grant confided to me

All evidence also says it was a success

Parsons opened a door and Something flew in

Any objective analysis

Of Western History since Jack's death

Must acknowledge the presence

Of his dark Elemental

Jung understood this Alien

As a collective mental delusion

Linked to the detonation of the atomic bomb

And oppression of the Individual

People see Outside

What they feel Inside

This Something flying in

Is the symbol

Of the Individual flying out

Of Human History

Elemental Darkness is the symptom

Elemental Darkness is the cure

To heal the World

I conjure a New Darkness

To overcome Jack's working

A New Babalon comes tonight

To bear my Moonchild

The prophets of Obedience

Moses

Jesus

Mohammed

Must now vanish

From the propaganda of the Apparatus

And affirm the value of Life

Something flew through Jack's door

It obscures the Light

It makes us flicker

Between Being and Non-Being

Between meaning and meaninglessness

It legislates the supreme social values

Of eating Modern Man

It develops the high technologies

Of excreting Modern Man

Only my New Man

My Terrorist

My Moonchild stands fast!

He's the Great Destroyer

And New Babalon is his mother

Listen to Jack

My joy is the joy of eternity

And my laughter is the drunken laughter

Of a harlot in the house of ecstasy

Yes!

Jack was blown to pieces

By his optimism and nonchalance

By his aristocratic style

The iron fist of Destiny

Cameron was beautiful

But she wasn't Babalon

Like Simon Magus

Presenting Helena to the Romans

She couldn't conceive

Or deceive herself well enough

To convince the Stars

It's all about your birthday Frank

The CIA believes your mother

Is the real Scarlet Woman

You were born in Pasadena

Nine months after the Babalon Working

They calculate your birthday

As a triple six

Certain renegade OTO members

And black psychological operators

Get off on numerology like this

They get off

And always get it wrong

Tonight we'll get it right

We'll conjure the New Babalon

Tonight we change the World!

We're superior to John Dee and Edward Kelly

Superior to Jack Parsons and Ron Hubbard

We're the Ilich Sanchez and Frank Glendover

Of our most astounding Intent

Seeking Consequence

Of the Truth of Ourselves

Forget the smell of the camels

The camel drivers

Modern Man

He prefers disinformation

And the resentful comfort

Of the Lie

Tonight we'll get it right!

I sing the Conjugation of Air

I sing the Invocation of Wand

I sing the Consecration of Air Dagger

As I masturbate to the east

Write down everything you see

No detail is irrelevant

No image too faint or fuzzy

Everything!

Frank turns away

Scanning the western sky

A falling star leads his eye to a yellow fire

Fifteen degrees above the horizon

Growing larger than a star

Larger than Venus

Larger than the Moon

It's the Sun

Out of Time and out of Place

Slinging massive arcs of magnetic fury

Frank's hypnotized

By its ancient and familiar Power

When Ilich comes a roar

The Sun morphs into Four

It's the face of a child

The Morning of the World

Then Two

It's the face of a maid

The Noontime of the World

Then Three

It's the face of a crone

The Evening of the World

And now he knows the answer

To Sphinx's riddle

Truth

Is

A

Woman

As Nietzsche thought

No matter what we imagine

Or conclude

Truth is a Woman

Enticing

Defying

Deluding

The Sun is One

Again

It's the Midnight of the World

Again

The Light is Black

Again

The Light takes human form

Again

She's dressed in Royal Spanish Crimson

She's holding her belly with both hands

She's approaching

Golden

Sweet

Secret

In seven seconds

Her womb expands full term

She blows him a Marilyn kiss

Yes!

The Moonchild!

Dessy's water breaks

And she goes into the final spasms of labor

Yes!

She's gone

Everything's gone

What did you see? asks Ilich

Breathing sharp and shallow

Nothing says Frank

I saw nothing

I've blinded myself

I've blinded myself looking at the Sun

It's the Oracle Frank

Once you know the Truth

You can never be hung

Every Present

Is opaque

Every Future

Transparent

Now we both fight blind

Here I Am says Frank

Groping in his backpack for the kit

I feel like I've been drifting in a starry cave

I feel like I've been crawling over seven continents of skin

I feel like I've been thinking in somebody else's brain

I'm ready says Ilich

Pressing his temple against the muzzle of the gun

Ulrike's at the hotel

She'll escort you back to the States

Santa Cruz is Colonus

She'll take good care of you

San Francisco is anxious for your return

I'm ready Frank

Do it

This is my Noble Death

The camel drivers have been told

Do what you're supposed to do

Pull the bloody trigger!

Frank laughs

Wheels

Fires one shot west

And drops the gun in the sand

I feel the Mountains Of The Moon massage my feet

I feel the Milky Way brush my cheek

What do you see?

The Identity of the Self

And the Identity of the World

Are decided by the circumstances of War

Between the Three Wills

As long as the Apparatus rules

We're all born in Exile

Our Thoughts

Our Emotions

Our Destinies

Are systematically denied

Their pure and natural expression

We live in total eclipse of First Will

But Life wins out

We go beyond Exile

We go through the Wall

We enter New Renaissance

The First unites with the Second

To overthrow the Third

The Apparatus falls within three generations

And the children of Athenapolis

Will tell the story of our struggles

To their children

Forever

I see the Mind of my Flesh

I see the Flesh of my Mind

We can't ask more of Vision than this

Ilich

Our Double Lives split here

Will Islam win the War?

Yes

Islam wins the War by losing the War

It accelerates the collapse of the Apparatus

By strengthening the Apparatus

Islam wins you by losing you

You have a daughter

But you desperately want a son

You're betrayed and captured in Sudan

During an operation to increase your sperm count

You convert to Islam in a French prison

Write a book on Islamic Revolution

Marry your French attorney

Ilich

It's been a great run

We meet and then we meet again

Now I take Responsibility

Now I go beyond Oedipus

Now every dawning day

Brings us closer to Athenapolis

Ilich

My friend

Our Double Lives split here

I owe you a large tin of Beluga caviar

I owe you a large tin of Beluga caviar

Contents

Page

1	That's The Way It Is
7	The Face Of Pythagoras
9	Spencer's Butte
15	The Comprehensives
17	Thanksgiving Light
22	The Recurring Dream
34	Windflowers
35	The Plastic Sax
37	The Smiley Introductions
41	Mustang Ranch
59	A Flamingo Lagoon
60	The Highgate Rumba
69	The Three Names Of Lenin
78	Letizia
81	Two Hours
82	The Logic Of German Girls
83	A Gentle Rocking Motion
89	Gertrude
92	The Piano
93	Red Flag Day
96	Near The Tibetan Border
99	Green Tea

Page

102 .... Too Much Nietzsche
110 .... Jack Parsons
119 .... Pontoon
120 .... A Small Gray
121 .... The Infinite Surf
122 .... Before Bali Rose Up Screaming
123 .... The Spike
124 .... Astrid
125 .... The Truth Rests In Turtles
127 .... The Thief
131 .... Pteripterix
134 .... Hit By A Thunderbolt
137 .... Crack
138 .... At The British Museum
139 .... The Kensington Gardens
153 .... Next Time You're In New York
157 .... Thirteen Steps To Hell
159 .... Underwater
160 .... Blues To The Moon
161 .... La Paz
164 .... Prodigal Sun
174 .... Gardena

Page

179 .... Over The Rim
185 .... Ulrike
191 .... The Job
197 .... Modern Man
208 .... The Vienna Raid
216 .... Lucky In Milan
219 .... Jose Altagracia Ramirez Navas
228 .... The Marks
233 .... The New Babalon Working

The Author

Lawrence Johns is a philosopher and poet, the inventor of Field Language and founder of Athenapolis. He is the author of a wide array of singular literary works. *Sensazioni*, his major revaluation of reading, is a history of consciousness written in a wordless version of FL featuring natural numbers.

Love And Hate, his epic poem on the rise and fall of Haight-Ashbury, was nominated for The National Book Award and The Pulitzer Prize.

Lawrence received his Ph.D. from The Graduate Theological Union.

He lives in Portland, Oregon.

The Conscious Libraries

The Classic Library

1. Science And Myth, Gianfranco Spavieri

2. Love And Hate, Lawrence Johns

3. Beyond Exile, Lawrence Johns

The Popular Library

1. The Golden Vortex, Nick Nelson

Conscious Publishing

2034 SW Vermont Street
Porland, OR 97219

www.consciouspublishing.com

*All Conscious Books,
including Special Editions,
can be ordered directly from our website.*

www.ingramcontent.com/pod-product-compliance
Lightning Source LLC
Chambersburg PA
CBHW060029180426
43196CB00044B/2053